AF480725

LIFE OF
THE PARTY

LIFE OF THE PARTY

*How Democrats Lost America's Trust —
and How They Can **Win It Back***

JOE CUNNINGHAM

SOUTH BATTERY
PRESS

TO DAD—my hero—who taught me that politics, at its simplest, is just about people.

TO MOM—for being tough and raising 5 boys to be the same.

TO ASHLEY—I love you to the moon! Thank you for supporting me every step of the way; and

TO BOONE & ALMON—I do it all for you.

CONTENTS

If your dreams do not scare you, they are not big enough.
—ELLEN JOHNSON SIRLEAF

While my phone buzzed in my hand, I stared at the area code of the incoming call. I didn't know anyone in San Francisco. Yet I knew exactly who was calling.

It was election eve in 2018 and I was sitting on top of the kitchen counter in the International Longshoreman's Association Hall downtown Charleston. A crowd in the hundreds stood on the other side of my door waiting for me to speak, a final "hoo rah" if you will, to help get out the vote and miraculously do something no Democrat had done in my lifetime: win South Carolina's 1st Congressional District.

It was ironic the call caught me at probably the only two minutes I'd had to myself in the previous several weeks of unrelenting campaigning. She of all people knew that timing was everything.

I swiped my iPhone and said "Hello."

"Joe, this is Nancy Pelosi. I wanted to congratulate you on a tremendous campaign down there," she started before continuing, "and when you win tomorrow and the lights come on and you begin your speech, just dive right into your vision and what you want to do for the district. Don't thank everyone in the beginning because the viewers at home will tune out. Thank your people at the end."

Probably good advice from a seasoned vet. I reasoned this was a courtesy call from the past and future Speaker of the House as polls showing Democrats were on the verge of taking over that chamber, transferring the gavel to her hands. She was laying the groundwork. Sowing the seeds of support for her new incoming freshmen House members, or at the very least, trying.

The call was brief and concise. Another name on her list, I figured. She did not ask for my vote then and I did not give her a "no." That was weeks away. As the call ended, my staff came through the door to tell me I was up next to speak. I hopped down and walked through the door. Hours later, I would be the first Democrat elected to South Carolina's 1st Congressional District in my lifetime. Weeks later, I would be speaking to Pelosi face to face.

It wasn't easy staring down a very nice lady, who was the most powerful woman in the United States. But, I kept my promise to the people of my district. I voted against Nancy Pelosi for Speaker of the House. I felt like the Democratic Party should be heading in a different direction. I still do. The brief history since that conversation has proven me right.

When I was seven, my older brother and I were playing on a dirt pile launching rocks across the street toward a neighbor's yard. Their house was set back a ways from the road and was safe from our developing muscles. After getting bored of launching projectiles into their yard, my brother dared me by saying I couldn't reach the side of the house. Taking his bet, I picked up a good-sized rock, got a running start, and heaved it across the road—and it sailed into the side of the home and straight through their kitchen window. We immediately scattered back home. When my dad returned home from work, it didn't take long for the news to reach him. The suspect list in our neighborhood was short and each name on it ended with Cunningham. He took me up to his room and sat me down on the edge of the bed. He didn't have to even tell me what I did for we both knew the charge. But he took a minute to let me know how much he loved me. How he only wanted the best for me. And how he wanted me to be the very best version of myself I could possibly be.

Then off came the belt.

I never threw another rock at a house. That is because I learned from a loving but disciplined home that the consequences of bad judgment can be painful. We learn to correct our behavior to avoid the same mistakes, the same pain, in the future.

The Democratic Party is currently suffering the consequences of our past mistakes.

I do love this party. I love it enough to speak hard truths, which, at times have cost me friendships, donors, and experiences.

I love it enough to say and do the things necessary to prevent it from self-destruction. These pages and chapters are written, like my father's punishment, without animus or spite. But out of a lifelong love affair with the Democratic Party.

Putting life back into our Democratic Party is a tough problem. But, as the saying goes, "to a tough steak comes a sharp knife."

1

POLITICS IN THE BLOOD

I would rather be a servant in the House of the Lord than to sit in the seat of the mighty.

—ALBEN W. BARKLEY

The tap root of my existence was watered by the Democratic Party.

I grew up in far west Kentucky, a rural area where four major rivers of the United States converge: the Mississippi, Ohio, Tennessee, and Cumberland.

My father's family has been there for centuries. It hasn't been easy for them.

At one time, far west Kentucky was the most impoverished section of one of the most impoverished states.

My grandfather once netted less than three dollars for a cotton crop. His father once refused to say grace before a meal, because he proclaimed that he was not thankful for the meager fare they had to eat.

During the Great Depression, times got even worse. Thousands migrated to the north to find jobs in Detroit and the booming automobile industry. My grandmother was the only one of nine children not to head north. She and my grandfather stood their ground, trying valiantly to grind out a living for their growing family on the land of their fathers.

Like most Southerners at the time, they were Democrats. Up until then, party affiliation and politics were seemingly of little importance. Then, the Democratic Party, through its champion, Franklin Roosevelt, came to their rescue.

In the first one hundred days of Roosevelt's administration along with a Democratic congress in 1933, there were wide sweeping actions taken to relieve Americans of our economic miseries. The Tennessee Valley Authority (TVA) was one of those programs. It not only built dams to electrify the homes in the mid-south, but they also enhanced the navigation along the Cumberland and Tennessee rivers. This incited river commerce to flourish, stimulating the economy in the rural areas of Kentucky and Tennessee, while also providing employment opportunities for the poor to escape the back-breaking and unprofitable farms to the better paying jobs of the river.

The leading political figure of those times in west Kentucky was Alben Barkley. He is a legend there and our biggest name on the national scene. This strong Democrat was Majority Leader of the Senate during the Roosevelt years and later vice president of the United States under Harry Truman. He was from far west Kentucky.

My impoverished and desperate grandfather became a "bathtub buddy" of the mighty Alben Barkley.

The story goes he had a boyhood friend and future Congressman, Frank Albert Stubblefield. Stubblefield was the county chairman for Barkley's bid for reelection to the Senate. One day Barkley was in my father's home county campaigning and was staying in the Murray Hotel in Calloway County. Desperate to leave the grinding poverty of the farm, my grandfather asked Stubblefield to intervene and see if Barkley could help. He wanted to join his two older brothers working on the river for the U.S. Army Corps of Engineers on a dredge boat. My grandfather had only an eighth grade education, and it looked like this was the only escape hatch from his existing plight.

Frank Albert dutifully went up to the Senator's hotel room and knocked on the door. He was ushered into the room by the aides. The Senator was in the bathtub. No matter. Barkley, the consummate man of the people, waved him in to take a seat on the commode. The great Alben Barkley listened intently as Frank Albert laid out the purpose of his mission. Barkley told his aides to jot down my grandfather's name and assured Stubblefield he'd see what he could do.

Two weeks later, my grandfather received a letter directing him to go to Paducah, Kentucky, and report for work on the dredge boat *Tishamingo*.

It was a letter that would change the lives of our family including lives in the future still unborn.

In his last days, dying of lung cancer, Stubblefield whimsically told my father, "Your dad was Alben Barkley's bathtub buddy." He would go on to explain. "On the next few occasions

I'd see Barkley, he would ask with a smile, 'How's my ol' bathtub buddy doing?'"

That was the wonderful age when government worked. It was the wonderful time when our Democratic Party was brimming with life.

And it was a moment when my family's devotion and loyalty to the Democratic Party became chiseled in stone.

My grandfather, Almon Cunningham, gratefully made the best of Senator Barkley's favor. He spent the better part of his life working on the water between western Kentucky and western Tennessee, and ultimately went to work on the locks and dams that TVA had strung up and down the Cumberland and Tennessee rivers. He even attained the position of lock master of the lock and dam located in Eddyville, Kentucky. It was the county where my father grew up. It was the county where I grew up. It was a career that provided my grandfather not only with a sense of pride, but a blanket of financial security that allowed him to raise four kids, including the youngest, Bill Cunningham, my dad. Where would we have been, where would I be today but not for strong Democrats Frank Albert Stubblefield, Alben Barkley, and the great Franklin D. Roosevelt?

Where would we have been without the Democratic Party?

My father drew me into politics. Back then it was called public service. He would say President John F. Kennedy was the inspirational force that called him to public service. After graduating from Murray State University, he went to law school at the University of Kentucky and was immediately drafted into the Vietnam War. He received a temporary deferment that allowed him to sit for the bar exam. If he passed, he would go in as an Army JAG officer. If he failed, he would go in as enlisted. Fortunately for him, he passed. Otherwise, there's a chance I would not be here.

After serving our country in Vietnam, Korea, and Germany, Dad returned to his small hometown of Eddyville to practice law. He would later become the city attorney, the commonwealth attorney, a circuit court judge and, ultimately, a Supreme Court justice for the state of Kentucky. All elected positions, all public service.

Looking back, I can draw a straight line between my desire to enter public service and what I learned from my dad. In a small town, it was impossible to go to the grocery, gas station or a restaurant without running into someone you know or, in his case, someone who needed help. For my dad, a trip to grab milk would turn into a conversation with a parent whose son had recently been arrested. Or a discussion with a person in the middle of a custody dispute. He was always on call and always available. He prided himself on having a published home number in the phone book. If people needed help, he would not hide. Because of this, calls would pour in at all hours of the day with the exception of dinnertime when my dad would take the phone "off the hook" to enjoy an uninterrupted meal.

I was the youngest of five sons. As such, I was the last one he could persuade to go on the campaign trail with him during those long summer days when school was out. I would travel across county lines to the BBQs, fried catfish dinners and other political events just to get a Blizzard from Dairy Queen at the end of the day, which he promised me. Being on the road with him gave me a front row seat to public service and the good that can come from it. It showed me what can happen when government works. Showing up, listening, and understanding people is the entire business of politics. Retail politics is defined as coming face to face with people where you feel their problems that resound through tone and emotions in one-on-one conversations.

While politics was part of my blood from early on, my practical side drove me to engineering. When I first got to college, I saw friends graduating with various degrees that enabled them to continue bartending or waiting tables. If I was going to spend the time and money in college, I wanted a degree that would afford me more options. I opted to transfer from College of Charleston to Florida Atlantic University to get my Bachelor of Science in Ocean Engineering. I was good at math, but not that good. In between waiting tables and living in the library I eked out a degree and later took a job over in Naples working for a marine and environmental consulting firm. It was an ideal job, and I was surrounded by great people while working on the water. The firm was charged with designing, permitting, and overseeing the construction of boat docks and marinas from south Florida to the Bahamas. However, I was about forty years too young for Naples, a town that is known for its bustling retiree population. After almost five years working as an ocean engineer, the recession that started in 2008 smacked south Florida hard. I was laid off and, with ballooning payments on my mortgage, was forced to list my house as a short sale to avoid foreclosure.

Thankfully, I was not married nor had kids. Otherwise, the situation would have been much worse. After losing my job, I gave much thought to finding another in the same field but couldn't muster the passion for it. I went on interview after interview talking with headhunters or business owners and listening to the job duties for which I could not get excited. I recall one job that was for a project manager of a low-level radioactive waste dump somewhere on the border of Texas and Mexico where I would have to undergo full body scans when leaving and entering the job site to ensure I wasn't being affected by the waste. It was at that point I realized I should turn elsewhere.

In the back of my mind was the business of people. Helping others. The practice of law had always been in my subconscious. Having grown up with a father who was always in and out of a courtroom, it was this setting I was drawn to. I loved the tales I heard from the extended lunches or late-night dinners where my dad and his colleagues would trade war stories from different trials. After leaving my job in Naples, I wanted to make a larger impact and, in my heart, that came not from working with concrete and steel, but with people.

I started law school in the fall of 2011 at Salmon P. Chase College of Law at Northern Kentucky University. I was twenty-nine years old. Entering a bit older afforded me more maturity, which helped me balance the studies with other obligations, like work.

While in school, I was employed by the Boone County Commonwealth Attorney's office, which is tasked with prosecuting felonies in Kentucky. There, I gained an immeasurable amount of experience in just less than two years. Indicting felons, working with police officers, and even trying a criminal case were just a few of the experiences I had. It was incredibly rewarding, and I understood why my dad called it the "most fun job" he ever had. Being in a courtroom was exhilarating. Most lawyers hardly stepped foot in a courtroom and I found myself in one several times a week.

Upon graduating from law school, I returned to Charleston, South Carolina, as my family had continued to accumulate there. My brother, Alec, and his wife and kids had been there since about the time I was in college. My brother Luke had relocated there and my parents eventually purchased a condo in the area. In the summer of 2014, I moved back and began the job hunt.

I needed a job, and my engineering background led me into construction litigation at a small boutique law firm in downtown Charleston. It provided me great exposure to the civil side of the practice as much of my time in the courtroom had been on the criminal side. However, it was mainly insurance defense. In this sector, attorneys are hired by the insurance companies to defend their insured. As such, most of your communication is with the companies paying your bills and that attorney-client relationship is not as personal as it would be if the individuals themselves hired you directly. The level of appreciation for legal services is not as high as it would be if the client hired you directly. Between that and spending most of my time looking at home construction defects, I found something lacking. I got into law to help others and I did not feel that itch was being scratched.

Then came the 2016 presidential election.

When people ask me why I got into politics, I have been able to shorten the answer considerably to say: Trump was elected and I overreacted. The longer answer is this. I recall going out for drinks on election night in 2016 with my wife and we were set to celebrate what we expected to be a stress-free victory. We cashed out before they had finalized the election results, but after the writing was on the wall. As we were going to sleep that night my wife asked me if Donald Trump was going to be our next president and I found myself in the position where I didn't want to give her a disappointing answer nor could I lie to her. My thoughts also wondered to my nieces who were young and how Trump's tone, words, and behavior would be normalized by his election. What would other boys say to my nieces and then get away with it simply because "The president is able to say those things." It set off an avalanche of thoughts that eventually led me to the question: What are you going to do about it?

I wanted to do something. I thought about later on down the road and what I would say if my son ever asked me what I did at this pivotal point in our nation's history. Making money, working, etc., did not seem like sufficient answers. The federal issues were the ones I was most interested in and they needed my attention. Solution: run for Congress!

Skeptical is the word I would use to describe how people felt when I told them of my plans to run for Congress. The 1st Congressional District was then held by former Governor Mark Sanford. Looking back, it was insane to even try to beat him. There were many Republicans who would have been vulnerable in a swing or purple district during Trump's first midterm election. But Mark Sanford was not one of them and the district was neither a swing nor a purple district or anything close to it. In 2016, Trump bested Hillary by thirteen points. Plus, Sanford was one of the few Republicans who would even consider voicing dissent with President Trump. In true Sanford fashion, he would not disparage or denigrate President Trump, but simply "respectfully disagree" when it came to a difference in tone or policy.

State Representative Katie Arrington had launched a long shot bid to upset Sanford. Despite Sanford voting with Trump over 90 percent of the time, she was able to successfully use Sanford's rhetoric against Trump to paint Sanford as someone unsupportive of the MAGA agenda. And it worked. On election night in June 2018, she did what many thought was impossible: defeat someone who had never been beat: Mark Sanford.

However, this upset would ultimately give rise to another: the race for South Carolina's 1st Congressional seat, which had just begun. Between June and November 2018, I campaigned on bridging the partisan divide and remained laser-focused on kitchen table issues. My opponent's support of President Trump lifting the ban on offshore drilling provided an opening I exploited. After all, protecting our shorelines was non-partisan and my opposition to offshore drilling allowed me to secure the endorsements of Republican mayors throughout the district. And late on the evening of election night—around 2 a.m.—the Associated Press called the race after I edged out my opponent by one point.

The local paper, *The Post and Courier*, called it "the biggest political upset in South Carolina history." *The State*, South Carolina's other premier publication, was so sure of Republican victory that they actually went to press late on election eve with a headline that Arrington had won, similar to the famous blunder by the *Chicago Daily Tribune* in 1948, which had printed "DEWEY DEFEATS TRUMAN."

The end of 2018 was spent assembling my congressional staff—both in DC and Charleston. And in 2019, I was sworn in to the 116th Congress of the United States. In the House of Representatives, the next campaign begins where the last one ended. In the 2020 election cycle, I went up against state Representative Nancy Mace who bested me by a point. Donald Trump was at the head of the ticket in a red state. It did me in.

By the end of April the following year, I had launched my bid for governor. In June 2022, I secured the Democratic nomination but fell short against incumbent Governor Henry McMaster.

Heading into 2023, I was equally surprised and disappointed that none of my colleagues had expressed the same hesitations I had about Biden's reelection. Everyone saw it. Everyone said nothing.

No Labels, a centrist organization and a nonpartisan group, had been tracking the discontent about the American public not only on Biden's decision to run again, but Trump's as well. I was familiar with the group that had focused mainly on Congressional issues and promoting bipartisanship. It had been instrumental in creating the Problem Solvers Caucus in Congress—a small group of half Democrats and half Republicans who met regularly to bridge the partisan divide. I was a member of the caucus in Congress and found it to be as effective as it was rewarding, even helping me build support for two of my bills that were eventually signed into law by President Trump. I had remained in contact with the group since leaving Congress and their efforts to give Americans another choice naturally piqued my interest.

By May 2023, I had officially joined No Labels to serve as their national director for the Unity Project. At this time, the Democratic and Republican parties were on their way to giving the country the Trump-Biden rematch that few Americans wanted. No Labels, through the Unity Ticket, was preparing to offer voters another option. The plan was to secure a place on the ballot for a bipartisan president/vice president if, and only if Americans wanted that option and if that option could actually win.

No Labels was not creating a third party, nor would it require any allegiance by potential candidates to another party. It would simply be a historical hybrid in highly dangerous and unusual times—a Democrat and Republican on the same ticket. My driving purpose was to keep Donald Trump from returning to the White House. At the time, it was all but certain both Trump and Biden would cruise through their respective primaries. Since Biden was not positioned to defeat Trump, another option was necessary.

So in May 2023, through an op-ed, I laid out the case, based upon empirical data, why Biden could not defeat Trump and why another option was necessary to do so. For the next year plus, the centrist group gained access to the ballot in many states and was prepared to give Americans another choice.

Ultimately, the group was unable to find the two leaders to fulfill the second half of that requirement, and so it suspended its efforts in April 2024. The unwanted rematch would continue until President Biden withdrew from the race on July 21, 2024. Vice President Kamala Harris filled his spot and the rest is history.

Unfortunately, the No Labels movement was exactly right. Biden was too old and stayed in the hunt too long. He hand-picked Harris, and he and our party shut down an open primary that would have given us a winning candidate against Trump.

So…here we are.

2

LESSONS IGNORED

The only real mistake is the one from which we learn nothing.
—JOHN POWELL

An older gentleman convinced his friend to go with him on a cruise. "It's a three-day cruise and only $150.00. You can't beat that deal!" he urged him. They were to meet down at C dock by the Wharf at 5 p.m. Sunday. They found themselves at the end of the dock waiting to embark when a loud smack was felt across the back of both their heads. Someone had knocked them unconscious, put them in a small boat and pushed it out to sea. A while later, both individuals started to wake. The younger one, rubbing the back of his head while taking in the scene, asked his friend, "You think they serve drinks on this cruise?" The older gentleman responded, "They didn't last year."

The Democratic Party refuses to learn from past mistakes. That's the first problem we have to face.

As we peer ahead to 2028 and beyond, I have great concern that the Democratic Party has not learned the lessons of the past few election cycles, especially 2024. I am unable to tell if the party even recognizes its faults or does recognize them and refuses to correct course. Unless there is a course correction soon, the party will find itself adrift in a vast open sea with a growing distance between themselves and regular voters.

While interviewing candidates for Democratic National Committee (DNC) Chair at a forum in January 2025, *Washington Post*'s Jonathan Capehart asks by a show of hands how many believe that racism and misogyny played a role in Vice President Harris's defeat. Every hand went up and Capehart responded, "You all passed." Following the 2024 election, the kneejerk reaction by national Democrats was to blame racism and sexism as the only plausible reason Harris could have lost. Talking heads on CNN and MSNBC were quick to fault the hatred of Blacks and/or women as the sole reason for her loss. However, blaming an entire campaign on gender and sex is intellectually lazy and it lacks any self-reflection. Moreso, it's not true.

Racism and sexism do exist in ample supply in our country. I am not denying that. Sadly, many Americans cast their votes based upon race and gender, much like they have in prior elections. However, I do not see this as a major factor in Harris's loss. Ironically, it was continuously calling people who supported

Trump racists and sexists that drove more people away from the Democratic Party.

On CNN's *News Night with Abby Phillips*, Republican pollster Frank Luntz stated that many Trump supporters feel "really, really tired of being accused of either racism or sexism because they voted for Donald Trump." Luntz is a very well-respected pollster and you would be hard pressed to find another who has spent more time with persuadable voters. These attacks continued to push voters—mainly white voters—away from Harris and toward Trump, even if they had to hold their nose while voting for him.

Barstool Sports' founder Dave Portnoy would later opine on why so many white men voted Republican in 2024. In an interview on *CBS Sunday Morning*, he said "And to be honest, the white guy, and this sounds—but, was the bad guy, became the bad guy," Portnoy continued. "And there's a lot of white dudes who are like, 'I'm not the bad guy. What are you getting mad at me for? I wasn't here for colonialism or any of the stuff you guys are complaining about two hundred years ago.'" His sentiment was widely shared.

A friend who is a white male sent me a text the day before the 2024 election, asking who I thought would win. I told him Trump. He responded, "Probably. Because of people like me. I dislike her just enough to overcome the embarrassment of voting for him." I knew when he said he disliked her, what he meant was he disliked all that went with her, like her surrogates, the activists, the left-leaning media, the liberal commentators who he felt were talking down to him. He, like others, were offended when they were painted as a sexist, racist, or bigot. He didn't like that so he was forced, grudgingly, into Trump's corner.

The national Democratic Party has refused to acknowledge their own self-inflicted wounds that led to their defeat.

Immigration was a consistent theme throughout the campaign. Border crossings increased significantly upon Biden taking office in 2021. Vice President Harris was appointed to assess the source of immigration, but Americans continued to witness illegal, dangerous immigrants pouring across the border. Stories of illegal immigrants committing heinous crimes and trafficking in dangerous narcotics concerned millions of Americans. When they turned to the Biden administration for answers or comfort, they found neither.

Many felt Biden abandoned the moderate Democrats in favor of the left flank. Social issues played a key role in cementing this sentiment, particularly issues surrounding the transgender community. In the last several years, progressives had been moving the treatment of transgender persons increasingly into the spotlight. To appear more inclusive, those on the left were changing their email salutations or business cards to include their pronouns. He/him. She/her. They/them. It was a tip of the hat to the transgender community. A sort of "we see you" to a group that had been historically marginalized.

Other conversations spawned off. Can a transgender use a bathroom not of their natural gender? Can a biological male compete in women's sports?

To please everyone, liberals ceded more ground to this community. In doing so we burned up a tremendous amount of political capital by catering to a sexual minority of about 1 percent of the population. My Democratic Party turned its back on the injustice that is being imposed upon all the parents and their teenage daughters who are being put at a biologically disadvantage by being required to compete against those who have male bodies. French writer Romain Gary summed it up well. "Liberals have a sense of justice bigger than anyone else, but not much of a sense of injustice."

Such positions of the Democratic Party are driving our members into the other camp in droves. They are becoming both angry and disgusted with what they see as the loss of rational thinking. Common sense has become a stranger in the House of the far left of the Democratic Party. While focusing on this very small group, the rest of Americans felt like government time and resources would be better spent on tackling issues like the cost of healthcare, insurance, groceries, and housing.

Perhaps the biggest failure was how Democrats ignored kitchen table issues. Between 2020 and 2024, the cost of housing increased by nearly 50 percent. Spending in healthcare increased each of those four years. Grocery prices increased nearly 25 percent during this four-year period. Auto insurance shot up by more than 50 percent and homeowners and health insurance increased as well. Wages failed to keep up with inflation during this period, and messaging from Democrats was noticeably void of any solutions. Even worse, the Biden administration attempted to convince Americans things were not so bad and that the economy was doing well. They rolled out a phrase "Bidenomics" that was poorly received and ultimately abandoned.

National Democrats pushed the above issues aside to focus on social issues. Much time was spent on talking about Trump's position on abortion. The Biden-Harris campaign was unable to craft any credible message on how they could reverse the Supreme Court decision that overturned *Roe v. Wade* and handed the issue back to the states. No Democrat could honestly say they would codify *Roe* through legislation because this would take sixty votes in the Senate and Democrats were far from that.

I believe that on the issue of abortion these decisions are best left between a woman and her doctor. I can also acknowledge that, no matter how important of a social issue this was, it was overshadowed by others, mainly economic issues.

Issues aside, 2024 was not a great year for the incumbency or the establishment. That's what Democrats were. Polling indicated that the majority viewed President Biden in an unfavorable light, partly because of the negative economic and security trends. When Biden stepped aside and endorsed Harris to be the Democratic presidential nominee, an opening was created for an agent of change. Yet, Harris missed the opportunity to distinguish herself from the unpopular administration in which she served.

On the television show *The View* one of the hosts posed the question to Harris: "Would you have done something differently than President Biden in the past four years?" The vice president's answer helped seal her own fate. She responded, "There is not a thing that comes to mind, and I've been a part of most of the decisions that have had an impact."

Some may chalk 2024 up as a bad election cycle. Others may claim President Trump was an anomaly and the race could not have been won. Those in the party who do not see a much larger problem at hand are untethered to reality. They haven't spoken with normal voters and fail to understand how actions and words of the national Democratic Party have repelled American voters. If there is no self-reflection, my fear is the Democratic Party will remain uncompetitive in all the red states.

In other words, if we change nothing, nothing will change.

German philosopher Nietzsche said—and I'm paraphrasing—"If you figure out the *why*, you can make it through any *how*."

We have failed to confront the question "Why did we get

Donald Trump? And why did we get him again?" To answer this question, you have to go back many years.

Enter Number 45.

Back in June 2015, Donald Trump descended an escalator in Trump Tower to announce his run for president. No one could have predicted the seismic shift that was about to occur in politics. As he waded into his announcement speech, he took direct aim at the immigrant community. He stated, "When Mexico sends its people, they're not sending their best... They're bringing drugs. They're bringing crime. They're rapists. And some, I assume, are good people." It was a line that would echo down the halls of the years and one that branded his future campaign.

Americans—including most Republicans—were frustrated with the state of our country. They had no place to direct that ire until President Trump provided them with a common enemy: immigrants. Anger was simmering across the country for various reasons. People feel they pay a lot in taxes and are reminded they do not get much in return. They drive on crumbling roads and depend on outdated infrastructure while sending their kids to under-performing schools and working a job that barely covers the cost of survival. The problems that led our country to this situation are complex and many, but Trump made it very simple: immigrants. And so started the politics of rage.

With the arrival of Trump on the scene, all of the energies and dreams of the Democratic Party have been drained away into anti-Trump phobia. Instead of fixing our own ship, and charting a course for a bright tomorrow, Trump's mean-spirited and divisive rhetoric and policies, lured us into a lunchroom food fight. We doubled our fists to fight Trumpism at every turn and in every speech and in every article…instead of opening our hands to build an alternative.

The result of our relentless battle wasn't just against Trump, it was also open warfare against the good Americans who voted for Trump. Hillary and Biden both disparaged Trump supporters personally. We became just like Trump. And in doing so and ignoring the causes of his popularity we got him elected president…twice.

The psychology of uniting a group against a common enemy is deeply rooted in evolution and sociology. The common enemy effect describes the social phenomenon where a group will unify whenever they face a shared adversary. If a "them" exists, a stronger "us" will, too. Perhaps one of the strongest "us versus them" moments in recent American history was after the terrorist attacks on September 11, 2001. Immediately following, America experienced an unprecedented swell of unity and patriotism. Eighty-nine percent of Americans reported they were "very proud" to be an American. President Bush's approval ratings surged to 90 percent, the highest ever recorded by a Gallup poll for any sitting president. It's hard to describe it to anyone who did not live through it. It epitomized the "us versus them" thinking and brought Americans from every single race, creed and age, and socio-economic status together to stand up against a foreign enemy. It wasn't the first time this has happened in our country either.

Going further back to the Cold War, this "us versus them" was deployed to push back against threats from abroad when American policies were largely shaped by the "threat of communism."

However, President Trump's "us versus them" message was multi-layered and not confined to just Americans versus immigrants. It was also Americans versus the political establishment. In his announcement speech in 2015, he proudly described himself as a political outsider, fighting against the establishment. In doing so, he connected with the frustrations simmering within Americans at a system that had continuously failed them.

Unfortunately for the Democratic Party, the *establishment* was synonymous with their party. At the time, the Democratic Party had held onto the presidency fourteen out of the last twenty-two years. It is easy to pin the problems on the party in power and Democrats had wielded more over the last couple decades when Americans had felt left behind. How President Trump—a billionaire—was able to connect so well with frustrated, working-class Americans with whom he shared little in common, will remain one of the greatest political feats in recent history.

The answer is simple: rage. Justifiable rage.

3

THE PRICE OF SURVIVAL

A nickel ain't worth a dime anymore. —YOGI BERRA

Something has happened in the last forty years or so. In our country, corporations and businesses have learned that a healthy profit can be made in the sectors that deliver necessities to Americans: housing, education, and healthcare. These are the pillars that hold up any developing nation. Greed has infiltrated each of them and made it harder for working families to survive, let alone thrive. If people can't go on vacation or purchase an ATV, they may be disappointed or slightly frustrated. But when they can't afford a home, medicine, or their child's tuition, primal instincts kick in.

In 2013, Martha and Richard Bray bought into a retirement community paying $314,000 for their townhome but were assured they would receive 85 percent of its value should they decide to ever leave. In 2023, after her husband passed, Martha was notified the community had been bought by private equity and their maintenance fee would be increased from $1,395 to $6,500 a month! She was told if she left, she would only receive 75 percent of the fee she had paid more than ten years prior. She was forced to move, losing over $100,000 during the process.

About one in every four homes are owned by investors. Realizing the incredible profits that could be made, private equity has taken hold of the housing market and used their leverage to drive up the costs on this basic human necessity. For example, a group called Blackstone has become the largest corporate landlord in the world, owning more than 300,000 residential units across the United States. By controlling that amount of volume, they are free to wield more control over rent prices than private owners. Private equity owns 1.6 million rental units across the United States, and a 2022 Congressional report showed they raised rents 7.5 percent annually as compared to 5 percent for non-private equity landlords. They also saddle tenants with more fees, which is essentially another way of raising the rent. A fixed fee for making a simple maintenance request, non-refundable pet deposits, monthly fees for online rent payment portal are just a few tools they use to gouge tenants for more money.

This isn't even the first time in modern history the entanglement between the housing market and equity groups has caused problems. Mortgage-backed securities, in which home mortgages are bundled and then sold as shares to investors, helped contribute to the housing collapse back in 2008.

Housing is the most expensive line-item families will pay every month. However, it is not the only necessary cost that is increasing and straining Americans.

The average price of prescription drugs has tripled just in the last two decades. The posterchild of the prescription drug hike was Martin Shkreli of Turing Pharmaceuticals who was nicknamed "pharma bro" for his smug, unapologetic demeanor after he acquired a drug used to treat infections and raised the price from $13.50 per pill to $750.

Even when private equity does not own the drug itself, they still find a way to inflate prices and line their own pockets. In 1990 a vial of insulin cost twenty-one dollars but by 2020 it had increased up to $350. This is because pharmacy benefit managers as well as other middle-men control the flow and price of drugs, much to the chagrin of working Americans. And Americans have felt the pinch. Two-thirds of all bankruptcies in America are because of medical debt. One in three GoFundMe campaigns are launched to cover medical expenses.

These are not just numbers, these are lives.

Alec Smith, a twenty-six-year-old in Minnesota began rationing his insulin because he could not afford the $1,300/ month price tab. As a result, he died of diabetic ketoacidosis. Many more are cast into financial ruin. Like Eric Smith, a landscaper from North Carolina who was bit by a snake, taken to the hospital and later received a bill for $89,000 for the antivenom administered. Drew Calver suffered a heart attack and was taken to an out-of-network hospital and later received a bill for $109,000. Stories like these are endless and you would not have to scroll far in your phone to find a loved one who has experienced the same.

As terrible as this situation has become, there's an even larger problem looming, which, if not harnessed and contained, will threaten the lives and safety of the ones we love most.

BIG TECH

In July 2020, sixteen-year-old Ayden Wallin from Colorado tragically died by suicide after discovering a website that promoted self-harm and learning about a product available on Amazon that he ultimately used to end his life. Just two months later, in September 2020, his mother, Meredith Mitchell, exchanged fifty-seven messages with Amazon, pleading for answers and accountability. Despite clear warnings and growing awareness that the product served no legitimate purpose beyond facilitating suicide, Amazon continued to promote, sell, and deliver it. The family's grief was compounded by the knowledge that this preventable tragedy was enabled—and that the company knew and did nothing.

A fifteen-year-old child with severe autism was lured onto Grindr, a hookup app, through campaigns on TikTok and Instagram where they use pictures of children in PE class and other places. Upon downloading the app, he was recommended to adult men and raped by four men within four days. In court, Grindr contended they had no duty to restrict children's access to their app.

Our kids are not safe online. They are given access to apps and websites they should not wander onto and become victims of predators that freely roam the halls of the internet. If there were continued reports of abuse at a playground, it would immediately be secured by authorities. Yet, because of an archaic law, Section 230 of the Communications Decency Act (1996), websites and tech companies are immune from responsibility for content they post or users they allow. Platforms have hidden behind this statute, claiming they cannot bear responsibility for bad actors who utilize their apps, even when these same companies profit off the same.

There are mounds of ongoing litigation against these social media apps and websites that have created unreasonably dangerous virtual playgrounds for our kids. Some school districts are taking matters into their own hands and doing what they can. At least eighteen states have effectively banned cell phones for kids in schools. It has been long overdue, and the sentiment has been overwhelmingly favorable. Teachers report their students are less distracted, are more focused, and they have noticed that the overall mental health of their students has improved. This was and is a political layup that can effectuate change and protect the health and safety of our kids. But raising our kids is not the jobs of teachers or administrators. That is up to the parents.

And parenting is a very difficult job. The challenges parents today face are significantly different than the ones our parents encountered. Back in the 1980s, less than half of married-couple households with minor children had both parents working. By 2020, up to 70 percent of these same households had both parents who were employed outside the home. Rising costs of living and wages that have not kept up have pushed both parents out of the house and into the work field to provide. As opposed to forty years ago, this dual income has become the norm and not the exception. This has placed additional strains on families—financial and emotional—and has yielded another unsustainable challenge to parents: the cost of childcare.

As new parents attempt to reenter the workforce, the

astounding costs of childcare in America is unrivaled. In most states, the average cost of childcare for two children exceeds the mortgage payment. In thirty-two states, it is cheaper to send a child to an in-state college than daycare. Between 1990 and 2024, the cost of daycare and preschool rose 263 percent. The costs are crippling young families who already struggle with inflation and the heavy cost of healthcare, insurance and housing. The result has been the gutting of America's middle class and the largest shift of financial wealth in our country's history.

People oftentimes misquote the Bible by saying, "Money is the root of all evil." But that's not true. In the first book of Timothy, it states, "The love of money is the root of all evil." It's an important distinction. There is nothing wrong with money as it can provide food, shelter, and comfort. Problems do arise when the pursuit—or love—of money become the sole focus and overshadow everything else, particularly a major lesson of Jesus: being kind to our neighbor.

I'm a capitalist. We live in a capitalist country. However, all our freedoms and liberties in America have some constraints and capitalism is no different. If corporations were allowed to operate completely unfettered, it would be ordinary consumers who would suffer the most. Like Isaiah Berlin said, "Freedom for the wolves has often meant death to the sheep." Some rules must be in place to ensure free markets survive. Afterall, if our economy is an engine, then competition is its fuel.

For several decades, we have witnessed a slow erosion of competition and an emergence of monopolies. But like a frog in boiling water, we have become too accustomed to the conveniences to notice the harmful impacts. It's easy to shop on Amazon, take an Uber or pay one bill for your cable, internet, and phone. As companies grow and merge, it is the stakeholders and board members who are the beneficiaries, not always the consumers.

This is nothing new.

Back in 1890, Congress passed the Sherman Anti-Trust Act, which was the first major legislative effort to curb monopolies and promote and preserve economic competition. At that time, large companies like Standard Oil, American Tobacco, and railroad companies were consolidating their smaller competitors into massive trusts that regulated prices and stifled competition. Ordinary and hard-working Americans suffered and after enough public outcry, Congress acted.

Since its passage, it's been used to break up monopolies and prevent companies from price fixing or dividing up markets. It has been strengthened by the Clayton Act and the Federal Trade Commission Act—both enacted in 1914, over one hundred years ago.

So how's that going for America? Not great.

In the health care sector, the sixty-nine-billion-dollar merger of pharmacy goliath CVS and health insurer Aetna was approved in 2018. That same year, health insurer Cigna and pharmacy benefit manager Express Scripts were approved for a sixty-seven-billion-dollar merger. How did this impact the consumer? Between 2018–2021 the number of pharmacies (i.e. competition) declined in forty-one states. In the last decade, drug prices have risen about 37 percent. Healthcare is a complicated industry and the above does not fully explain why we pay more for medicine than any other industrialized nation. But it is easy to see how this doesn't help competition and, as a result, harms capitalism.

In 2016, the Anheuser-Busch InBev + SABMiller merger

was approved, which included beers like Budweiser, Bud Light, Stella, Corona, etc. Afterward, consumers saw prices go up 6 to 10 percent while small brewers struggled to compete with distribution. The list goes on and on for products we put in our bodies, as well as the information we consume.

Back in 2019, the largest U.S. newspaper chain, Gannett, merged with Gatehouse Media and now controls about one quarter of newspapers circulated in our country. Because of consolidation and other factors, more than a quarter of all newspapers have been put out of business in the last two decades. More than two hundred counties in our country have no local newspaper at all.

Uber's average ride price increased 30 percent from 2018 to 2019. From 2019–2022, it increased another 41 percent. Not surprisingly, their market dominance has also increased during this same time.

Anti-trust laws focus a lot on mergers and monopolies. Conspiracy is also an enemy of capitalism, and the free market and rapidly developing technology has yielded numerous ways companies can exploit their consumers.

Have you ever gone online to check the cost of a plane ticket only to return the next day (or even hour) to find out the fare has increased? Dynamic pricing is one of the reasons you may see fares or prices increase on something like a plane ticket, hotel, or concert ticket. Or a surge on a ride-share platform. Supporters may argue this is simply a part of supply and demand, yet it creates a good deal of frustration for consumers who feel businesses are not being transparent.

That frustration felt by consumers does not necessarily mean it is illegal. Legal dynamic pricing occurs when companies respond independently to market signals, like plane tickets on holidays, surges with Uber, etc. It crosses the line into illegal behavior when companies begin using non-public competitor data or colluding with others in the industry to coordinate prices. The latter drives up prices and can really hit home for Americans. Literally.

U.S. Attorney General Pam Bondi stated, "Nowhere is competition more important than in making housing affordable again." This followed a settlement in which America's largest landlord, Greystar, agreed to stop using algorithmic rent-setting software that prosecutors alleged could violate price-setting laws. Greystar, which manages nearly one million rental units, was using rent-setting algorithms by a group called RealPage, a Texas-based software company that was also sued by the DOJ.

Whether it's in a smoke-filled room with CEOs or through computer software, price setting is illegal and undermines capitalism. Technology is advancing at warp like speed, harvesting data Americans surrender unwillingly and unknowingly. It has made lives easier in some respects yet created opportunities for economic exploitation by nefarious actors. If the middle class is to survive—and capitalism preserved—our anti-trust laws will need to be revisited to reflect the times in which we live.

How much Americans are paying for livability is a huge frustration. Equally frustrating is how they are being treated. Even before COVID, the customer experience has been less than satisfactory; however, since then things have only worsened.

Many companies cannot be reached on the telephone and have instead substituted AI chatbots to deal with customers. Phone operators have been replaced by chatbots of endless FAQs you must navigate. A 2024 study reveals that 70 percent of companies are prioritizing such digital channels over phone numbers. The larger the company, the less likelihood you will be able to find assistance with a pulse. Businesses that advertise with Google or Meta are unable to speak to a live person who can answer basic questions.

Some of the larger corporations that have drawn the ire of the general public are airline companies. With the merging of different airlines, there are now four companies that control 80 percent of the air travel market in the United States. During this time, seat space has decreased while passenger density has increased resulting in a growing frustrated class of air travelers. Compound this with increasing delays and cancellations, it has made air travel a wretched experience for many.

To address this, former President Biden proposed a rule that would have compensated passengers $200–$300 for delays of two to three hours and up to $775 for longer disruptions. It was an incredibly populist rule, which may have benefited him more if it had garnered more attention. The Trump administration has since scrapped this idea. If your flight has been delayed or cancelled, it is upon you to navigate the labyrinth of webpages to find out where and how you can receive reimbursement for travel expenses. Very easy for these companies to take your money, yet very hard for them to return it.

All these woes could just be chalked up under capitalism and allowing the free-market to be free. However, when these same industries come crawling to the government for financial bailouts, higher expectations should be set when it comes to customer service. During COVID, major airlines received billions of tax dollars to keep their operations afloat. Since emerging from COVID, demand for travel has resulted in higher profits for these companies, yet the quality of service to customers—the same taxpayers that carried them through tough financial times—has only worsened.

While the severity or importance of all these issues may vary—from the necessity of healthcare to the amenity of air travel—the theme remains the same. Americans are bearing the increasing cost that yields record profits for companies that face limited competition. All the while, the recourse for grievances of these same customers has all but been eliminated. People were angry. People remain angry.

It's the sentiment the Democratic Party has largely failed to appreciate. The frustration has been growing like a steady drumbeat for years and years, but the Party has not heard it.

Simply because it has not been listening.

4

LISTENING IS LEADERSHIP

We have two ears and one mouth so that we can listen twice as much as we speak.

—EPICTETUS

Dale Carnegie's *How to Win Friends and Influence People* is the gold standard of self-improvement books. I've read it multiple times. It has sold more than thirty million copies for one sole reason: it works. In it are lessons relating to how to approach and deal with people, particularly those with whom you may not always agree. One section addresses an often-overlooked attribute for effective leaders: listening.

Listening is a trait that eludes most people, especially

politicians. Those running for or holding office are more preoccupied with telling you what they think or how you should think. They rarely stop and listen to what you think and why you think it. If they did, their messaging would be better crafted to reflect the needs and desires of voters.

Back in 2021 when President Biden's first midterm was upon us, the question that rested in the back of everyone's mind was "Is he *actually* going to run again?" Although the query had not been brought to the forefront of cable news, it was just on the horizon. It was also during my gubernatorial primary and I had begun a forty-six-county–wide tour of South Carolina. The goal was to touch every corner of the state and listen to the needs of our residents. It was an ambitious one, although perhaps not so much compared to larger states like Texas and California. This tour would allow me to see parts of the state I had not seen. The district I represented in Congress consisted of parts of five different counties, all situated along the coastal area known as the Lowcountry. The main point of the tour was to listen.

As a candidate, you always enter a race with topics that you wish to discuss. These are policies that are personal to you and it is easy to believe others feel similarly. Then you find that while some agree with you on the existence of the problem and perhaps even the solution, it is not a top priority for them. Therefore, it is not a matter that influences their vote.

There are also issues that empirical data indicates are important to voters and would sway their vote. There is also the anecdotal evidence, which is gathered straight from the voter's mouth. There is no substitution for the latter. Rubbing elbows while discussing everyday problems is the best way for one to gather such anecdotal evidence that can help hone the message.

Whether or not Biden should seek out another term was a question I posed in every county I went during my statewide race. This was during my primary, so everyone I spoke with were engaged and reliable, primary voters. They were strong activists and/or party chairs for their respective community. I asked the question and, unsurprisingly, nearly everyone agreed that he should pass the torch.

But they remained as quiet as a midnight graveyard.

Why was there such a disconnect between how Democrats felt and how Democratic leaders spoke? How was it that most Democrats wanted another option and felt Biden was too old to run, yet no Democratic leader would stand up and translate that sentiment into words? The answer was our Democratic leaders were not listening. It could not be that voters were not talking, because poll after poll consistently stated another Democratic leader was desired.

Media pundits would tirelessly defend Biden's record. "No president has ever accomplished what he has in two years." "He's been nothing but bipartisan." "He has a better record than any president in modern history." These pundits and politicians were not listening. It was not about his record or accomplishments. It was about him and mostly his age.

One can applaud Biden's achievements yet still recommend he stand down in the next election. Whether he has done the job and whether he can continue doing the job are two different questions, and Biden's supporters were answering the former instead of the latter.

I would love to believe this was innocent and a careless mistake. With more time passing, I cannot help but feel there was a sense of arrogance from the leadership within the Democratic Party that forced this error in judgment. To counter the public numbers on Biden's performance, elected Democrats and left-leaning mouthpieces for the national media would often retort, "Well, it's still early and no one is paying attention yet." Or "Wait till we remind voters what Biden has done and then they will change their mind." The early warning signs were present, but most Democratic leaders had their heads stuck in the sand. Some were trying desperately to convince voters how delicious the dish is when those same voters made it clear they had no appetite for another four years of Biden. It was as if the left-leaning media or Biden's surrogates were more focused on protecting Biden than protecting democracy.

When I became the first Democrat calling for Biden to step aside, it was not done rashly but after long conversations with voters. I learned they felt the same way I did. That sentiment was widespread. That is what comes from listening.

Asking questions and being inquisitive not only serves politics well, but many other professions, too. In most depositions I attend as an attorney, one of the last questions posed to the party being deposed is "Is there anything else I did not ask you that you'd like to say?" This can be like pulling a pin from a grenade and waiting. If a person takes this bait and starts up, you'd better buckle up because what comes out can be some of the most useful information you will acquire. Responsible reporters do the same thing at the end of their interviews. "Well, is there anything I missed that you'd like to add?" This was a great way to slide in any messaging points if the reporter did not ask you directly. It's also a good way to get off message and go off on a tangent if you are not disciplined.

For any seasoned politician, listening provides the best first-hand account of how policies or ideas impact the lives of their constituents. When it comes to powerful and emotionally charged stories, there is no replacement for anecdotes you gain while listening.

During the statewide tour in South Carolina, I found myself one rainy evening in Calhoun Falls, a town with less than two thousand people situated in the upper northwest corner of the state. In a small community center, we all found shelter from the poor weather and discussed national politics as well as their community's pressing desires. When I asked their young and engaging mayor what their community most needed, without hesitation he responded, "A grocery store." He said there was not one grocery store nearby and that his constituents are forced to cross county lines to acquire essentials.

It brought me back to the rural area I grew up in.

Bill Martin's CB grocery was the local market in my small town of Kuttawa, Kentucky. We knew everyone there and they knew us—my parents and their five boys, with me the youngest. One day when I was about five years old, my mother got a call from the store manager advising her that her youngest son was attempting to cash a million dollar check for a pack of gum and was demanding his change. The check had been drawn on Marie Duncan's checkbook that my older brother Alec had uncovered rummaging through her burn barrel in her back yard. Alec went on a lavish spending spree, cutting checks to all his friends, making bets and, ultimately, paying his youngest brother to take over his household chores. It all caught up with him when my mom got the phone call and was forced to retrieve her youngest in the grocery store manager's office. It goes without saying I was more than upset.

That grocery store in my small town provided nearly every-thing we needed. And even things we did not. During summer break, we would dodge the heat and go in there and cool off, purchasing candy and packs of Topps baseball cards. It was always disappointing that none of the packs contained any valuable baseball cards. But it made sense years later when we found out the two guys working in the butcher department had been opening those packs for years. They would cherry pick the cards with any value. Then they would use the hot sandwich press to seal the plastic sleeve back together.

It's not only groceries people get at small town stores. They interact with people they love, accumulate lasting childhood memories. The grocery becomes a working community center and a part of growing up. So it touched me when I learned they didn't have a grocery, and it wasn't hard for me to imagine how the existence of one could change the face of a small town.

For the fine people of Calhoun Falls, it wasn't inflation, crime, foreign wars, abortion, or transgenders that loomed first on their list. It was the need of a grocery store.

The plight of Mayor Holland is familiar throughout South Carolina and the South in general. Had I not traveled to Calhoun Falls, put my boots on the ground, asked questions and listened, I never would have known the issues that are personal to that community. And it was remarkably simple and a story I carried with me throughout the campaign. Politicians oftentimes spout their ten-point plan or policy to address whatever ailment he or she thinks a town has, when what a person or community may need most is as simple as a grocery store.

How could I have helped? I didn't know. But I was gonna try. I listened.

While serving in Congress I wanted to be mindful of making things local and personal when addressing challenges. So, if I were speaking in one town about the need for better roads or highways I would make an effort to call out by name the bridge that requires repair or the specific road widening project that was long overdue. I would not know these things had I not listened. I picked up these nuances that would later connect me with my constituents.

To listen to voters, you also need to show up. Few politicians face the heat because they serve in safe seats that are gerrymandered to their respective parties. I attended a town hall that then Congressman Mark Sanford had held at a local government building. It was back in 2017 and Congress's umpteenth effort at repealing the Affordable Care Act. I showed up at the town hall an hour early expecting to snag a good seat but when I arrived, there was a swarm of people outside and we were notified all the seats had been taken. Folks outside were frustrated and moments before the scheduled town hall Congressman Mark Sanford showed up and was informed the event space had completely filled up.

"Listen up, everyone," he said outside the building while holding his hand up to get the attention of all concerned voters who had shown up that Saturday morning. "I've been informed that inside has reached its capacity, so what we will do is I'm going to talk to these folks inside and answer their questions and then I'll come out here and answer yours."

I hung around outside and true to his word, Sanford finished up inside and came outside. He spoke for twenty minutes and then took questions. Every one of them. As I was driving out of the parking lot, I looked over and saw Sanford speaking with the last two remaining citizens. Despite what answers he may have given, showing up spoke volumes for Sanford. He knew what public servants are supposed to do.

Years later, I would be planning my own town halls and showing up even in the most uncomfortable of times and places. During the Mueller investigation, I was regularly holding townhalls across my district on the weekends. In a district that overwhelmingly supported Trump, those conversations can be challenging. I learned that it's not your supporters who show up at town halls. They're with their kids at soccer practice or they are out enjoying their weekend. They are happy with the job you're doing and have no grievances to air. It's mostly those who are displeased with you or your political party. That was the case at all of mine that were frequented with red hats and MAGA signs.

You do enough townhalls and you learn the subtleties of them. How the location and length of them impacts the crowd size. How having someone hold the microphone for the person asking questions ensures they don't monopolize the conversation. Most importantly, town halls were always a reminder that your neighbors are genuinely good, decent Americans with whom you simply have disagreements. Yet, you strive to find some common ground. In other words, it's a reminder to empathize.

Showing up matters. Voters crave accessibility. Even when something as intimate as a town hall is not possible, they expect questions answered via interviews. In the 2024 presidential race, the decision to avoid the press by the Harris campaign proved detrimental. During the first fifty-nine days of her campaign, she and vice presidential nominee Tim Walz conducted a total of seven interviews and press conferences with TV and print reporters. Compare that to more than seventy conducted by Trump and Vance during that same time span. Avoiding your voters in a personal setting like a townhall and avoiding them on camera via the press sends many negative messages. It insinuates you're above any questions or concerns by the public or that you cannot be held accountable for your words or actions.

Dodging the press also sends the message that you're

unreachable. Americans like accessibility. MSNBC host Stephanie Ruhle described a time days before the election when she dialed Trump's cell phone and was able to speak with him. She contrasted that with the extreme difficulty (or impossibility) she experienced when trying to do the same with Harris or Biden. "But the reverse of that, if I were to want to connect with Vice President Harris or President Biden, there's fifty people between me and that I could write a note that maybe could get to somebody to get somebody then through Pony Express and a pigeon, something might end up in a mailbox near them," she said. Ruhle was giving credit to Trump for at least being accessible, which is an attractive quality that voters look for in their elected officials.

Showing up leads to listening. American playwright Wilson Mizner said it simply: "A good listener is not only popular everywhere, but after a while he gets to know something."

Listening naturally leads to the next emotion that determines whether you have their support: empathy. Support for Democrats has, in recent elections, waned and most polls suggest the party has become out of touch. They feel Democrats do not understand the struggles most Americans face. Or simply, the party lacks empathy. This is not an emotion one can fabricate. It is either real or not and voters can tell the difference and then vote accordingly. The business of politics is filled with all sorts of personalities, yet those who succeed are more often those who can connect and empathize with their constituents. If showing up or being accessible is the left shoe, then empathizing is the matching right shoe.

Despite Trump's flaws, and there are many, he has been successful in connecting with his supporters by tapping into their frustrations and connecting with them on an emotional level. But what does it say about the Democratic Party when a billionaire is more successful connecting with people on an emotional level than the supposed "Party of the working class?"

During the 2024 election, the Biden campaign, and later the Harris campaign, was quick to dismiss the legitimate and genuinely held concerns of millions of voters. In mid-2023, President Biden introduced the term "Bidenomics" to paint his economic policy, attempting to persuade Americans the economy was in fact doing well. He would point to the low unemployment rate, declining inflation and other metrics to make his case but the American public remained unconvinced. Americans looked at the cost of milk, eggs, and rent and were less persuaded by a jobs report or unemployment rates. But instead of listening, and empathizing, Biden was just lecturing them on how they were wrong and that things were all right.

The Democratic leadership became the swindlers of the 1837 classic fairytale by Hans Christian Anderson "The Emperor's New Clothes." They fooled the emperor and themselves. But when exposed of their nakedness in the November 2024 election, they did not fool most of the American people.

The Biden-Harris administration's failure to listen to voters on economic concerns was, in my opinion, a large contributing factor to their loss. Even after Harris was defeated by Trump, the administration still did not change course. In a post on January 15, 2025, just days before Trump was sworn into office, the White House's official Instagram account posted a split screen with two different headlines. On the top part and under the title "How it Started" is a headline from *Forbes* saying, "Biden is inheriting one of the worst economies in recent history." Under the "How it's going" part of the screen is another headline from *The Wall Street Journal* that reads, "The next president inherits a remarkable economy." It was a not-so-subtle pat on the back to their administration for their supposed remarkable economic policies.

At the time, as was during the campaign, Americans were incredibly frustrated by the cost of housing, healthcare, and groceries and did not share the sentiment of *The Wall Street Journal* or Biden's staff that the economy was doing great. Once again, an example of not listening to voters, but simply telling them how to feel or think.

The same strategy was deployed on the issue of immigration. Despite Americans' widespread concern on border security, the Biden campaign waited until mid-2024 to begin acknowledging it was an actual problem. It wasn't until June 2024 that his administration issued an executive order partially suspending asylum requests at the southern border. Harris's track record on the same issue was equally unimpressive. In March 2021, Biden tapped her to lead the effort in tackling the issue of immigration and determining the root causes. Yet months after she was given the task, Harris was pressed by NBC's Lester Holt on why she has not yet visited the southern border.

"At some point, you know, we are going to the border," Harris told Holt when asked if she plans to visit the border. "We've been to the border. So this whole thing about the border. We've been to the border. We've been to the border."

"You haven't been to the border," Holt responded.

"And I haven't been to Europe," she replied. "And I mean, I don't…understand the point that you're making."

This exchange highlighted not only the mistake of not showing up but also dismissing the real concerns that so many Americans had of border security.

The casual dismissal of issues with the southern border has

not been limited to Biden and Harris. New York has seen a surge in immigrants in recent years, and New York City has been struggling to keep up with the influx and the strain it places on local resources, including public safety. But on December 22, 2024, New York Governor Kathy Hochul tweeted pictures of herself on the subway touting how her policies have made the mass transit system safer.

"In March, I took action to make our subways safer for the millions of people who take the trains each day," Hochul's post read. "Since deploying the @NationalGuardNY to support @NYPDnews and @MTA safety efforts and adding cameras to all subway cars, crime is going down, and ridership is going up." Just eight hours prior, a migrant from Guatemala allegedly set a woman on fire and watched her burn to death on an F train in Brooklyn. The poorly timed tweet highlighted the disconnect between the Governor and reality.

Telling someone they should feel safe when they don't, or that the economy is doing well when it isn't, is a losing strategy because it omits the element of empathy and replaces it with arrogance.

We all have our own life experiences to draw upon that help us better understand the plights of everyday Americans. It is easier to connect with a person who voices their concern if you, personally, have been impacted in a similar way.

My four brothers and I all attained college degrees by taking out student loans. After some years of struggling, all five of us paid off our student debt. One of my brothers used his inheritance from our grandmother to pay off the loan. As the youngest, I was a United States congressman and still making payments. We had this strange notion that it was the honorable thing to do. Being saddled with student loan debt gave me a deeper appreciation for the heavy burden it places on young Americans. It wasn't until I was forty-two when I completely paid off my loans from undergraduate and law school. Yet, that experience gives me not only the credibility to talk about this critical issue, but the empathy needed to connect with those similarly situated.

It's easier to relate to skyrocketing housing costs if you've experienced it. Upon graduating with my degree in Ocean Engineering in 2005, I proudly purchased my first home. Like millions of Americans though, I found myself underwater on the home and was ultimately forced to sell it to avoid a foreclosure action. It was emotionally exhausting going through that process and losing a home I had worked hard for, spending countless days and dollars renovating only to lose it due to the cratering of the housing market. It was a hard life lesson. However, it was one that allowed me to better understand those who were pinched or crushed by the increase of rent, interest rates and home prices.

Out-of-control costs in healthcare are another threat Americans face every day. Following the delivery of my second son, Almon, my wife Ashley and I stared down the endless bills that arrived from the hospital for the cost of delivery. We spent hours upon hours calling our insurance carrier and the medical providers to sort through and settle the debts accrued. The whole process placed a dark cloud over what should have been one of the most important and joyous moments in life. Exorbitant medical bills are now the leading cause of bank-ruptcies for Americans. While it is not completely necessary to experience this firsthand to fully understand the issue, it certainly makes it easier.

The gap between voters and the Democratic Party may have grown, but it can still be bridged because the answer does not cost one penny. And everyone is capable of doing it. It's just listening and there is no excuse why Democrats cannot do it. Showing up where voters are so they know we are concerned and empathize is critical to earning back their trust.

Regaining the trust of the voters is inarguably the largest challenge ahead for the Democratic Party. But not all is lost.

5

RESTORING CREDIBILITY

Trust, once lost, could not be easily regained. Not in a politician, and not in a democracy.

– BARACK OBAMA

Aristotle outlined three elements to winning an argument, which he described as ethos, pathos and logos. Ethos focuses on the speaker's credibility to bolster their argument; pathos is a way to appeal to the emotions of an audience; and logos will appeal to their reason and logic by the use of facts.

You've seen the ethos leg of this stool on display in media, both TV and print.

"Joining us now to discuss this national security issue is former

CIA analyst. . ." Or the headline, "I'm a marriage counselor of forty years, this is the number one reason why couples divorce." These intros are intended to bolster the speaker's credibility by highlighting their ethos or ethics, which, in turn, make you more likely to believe what they say. Thus, attacking another's ethos undermines the credibility of a person. Or a political party.

During Season One of the 2024 presidential election when Biden was running as the nominee, the message of the campaign was "Save Democracy." A second Trump term, Democrats warned, would be the end of democracy as we knew it and no one would ever have the chance to vote again as the country would fall into a dictatorship.

How well was that message received? Well, numerous polls showed that both parties were effectively even when it came to trust.

Allow that to sink in. With polling on the issue of "saving democracy" essentially dead even between Democrats and Republicans, the former were placing all their eggs in that basket. Compare that to the issue of immigration with which Republicans had a twelve-point advantage over Democrats when voters were asked who they trusted more on this issue. If those numbers were dead even, do you think Republicans would be investing every last drop of funding into amplifying that issue? Or would they have picked another of which they possessed a commanding lead over their opposition? You know the answer. The Republican Party would either adjust the narrative on immigration or pick a completely different issue to anchor their campaign, preferably one that creates some distance from the Democratic Party.

So why did the message of "save democracy" fail to carry the day?

The reason many Americans do not trust Democrats is because of what they have seen with their eyes and heard with their ears.

President Biden was elected in 2020 under the promise he would be a bridge to the next generation. He implied he was to be a transitional figure, serving only one term. A year or two into his first term, it was becoming apparent he was ramping up for another election. Despite the clear message being delivered via polling, telling him not to run, he plowed ahead. In the face of historically low approval ratings and nearly two-thirds of Democrats not wanting him to run, he decided to seek reelection. What followed led to a series of events that will tarnish the credibility of the Democratic Party for years to come.

It is not uncommon for an incumbent, even a president, to receive a primary challenger. With Biden's low approval numbers, more were stepping up and quickly learning the big tent wasn't so big. Robert Kennedy, Jr., a legacy name in the Democratic Party and a person with a colorful and oftentimes controversial past, stepped into the fray. Kennedy had just enough clout to be taken seriously by the Democratic Party. This was not a nobody. It was an opponent Biden either had to deal with directly or ignore and hope he would fade into the background. To his detriment, the Biden campaign chose the latter. Like most primary opponents challenging an incumbent, Kennedy struggled to get oxygen. Television stations, particularly those on the left, did not book him or cover his campaign and the issues on which he ran. Meanwhile, he also struggled with ballot access. Kennedy maintained the DNC and other state parties were continuously moving the goalposts and blocking him from getting his name on the ballot.

He was not alone.

Minnesota Democratic Congressman Dean Phillips spent weeks pleading for other well-known and better funded Democrats to wade into the primary so voters could have the choice they so clearly wanted. Finally, in October 2023, Phillips announced his own primary challenge to Biden. He would come to learn some hard lessons on going up against the big muscle of the national party and what consequences there are for challenging the elites. Dean was blocked from getting his name on the primary ballot in North Carolina and Tennessee. In Florida, the Democratic Party cancelled their primary, effectively blocking him from the ballot there. In Wisconsin, he had to appeal to the Supreme Court to get on the ballot. Were all these states operating in isolation or concert? Were there efforts to block him from the ballot part of a broader scheme to stifle competition?

Neither Kennedy nor Phillips were ever given the opportunity to debate Biden. This form of campaigning—*ignoring your competition and not giving them any oxygen*—has worked in the past. It's the playbook an incumbent uses when their challenger has no money or name recognition. Yet, this was different. Both candidates could be viewed as credible. Kennedy, even with his baggage and dual positions, was an accomplished attorney from a political dynasty. Dean Phillips was a successful businessman and a sitting Democratic congressman. Perhaps more importantly, both challengers—like most Democrats and even Americans—yearned for someone other than Biden. The consequences of ignoring both of these primary challengers could prove to be detrimental.

On October 9, 2023, Kennedy switched his affiliation to Independent and continued his run for president under a different banner. He was still attacked by Democrats and Democratic-aligned groups who sued to keep him off several ballots for fear he would throw the election to Trump.

"RFK Jr. was recruited to run by MAGA Republicans; is being propped up by Trump's largest donor; and his own campaign staff has said their goal is to hurt President Biden," said Matt Corridoni, a spokesperson for the Democratic National Committee. This was a narrative that would persist through the remainder of the election cycle.

Frustrated by the lack of traction and institutional impediments, Phillips ended his campaign on March 6, 2024.

If the Biden campaign had given both (or either) of these candidates the credibility they deserved, one of two things would have happened. In one, Biden could have welcomed a robust primary and discussion on the issues. A lively campaign might have ensued in which, upon seeing a vigorous Joe Biden defend his rhetoric and prosecute the case for a second term, voters might decide he was the man for the job, again. Or an exhaustive campaign, coupled with one or two public debates, might lead Americans to the conclusion that Biden was not up for the job and a new nominee was needed to "defend democracy." Or an open field may have freed up an entirely new pool of Democratic candidates from which our great hope might ride upon the scene.

After exiting the primary, Kennedy went on to support President Trump and gave his supporters a place to call home. Had Biden welcomed Kennedy into the primary process and simply dispatched of him, perhaps it would have been one less headache for Biden at the end of the day. By ignoring Dean Phillips, the national Party was ignoring the message he carried: that the Party wanted another choice. More consequentially, by ignoring Dean's message, it was not listening to their own voters. And that was possibly the largest error.

No Labels, founded over twelve years ago, is a 501c4 that advocates for bipartisanship and commonsense solutions in

Congress. They helped form the Problem Solvers Caucus, a group comprising half Democratic members of congress and half Republicans. I was asked to join in 2019 and discovered it was one of the few places in DC that put both parties in a room to address the nation's pressing issues and possible solutions. The two bills I introduced, which made it through a divided Congress and ultimately got signed into law by President Trump, would not have been possible without the support of this caucus.

No Labels' time and energy was spent on supporting the caucus and its members and fostering conversations with members of Congress and those active in their community. While No Labels work had been traditionally focused on Congress, that shifted in early 2023. As a repeat between Biden and Trump appeared inevitable, the exhaustion of the American public was palpable. And No Labels' knew it.

So the group began modeling and collecting data to determine if an independent, bipartisan ticket might have a pathway to victory in the 2024 presidential election. When polling and focus groups suggested it was, the group began to pursue a place on each state's ballot for president/vice president. That slate would run if: Americans wanted a third option and if the No Labels' ticket had a path to victory in the electoral college.

It was becoming more evident that the national Democratic Party was dead set on a binary election, even when the public wasn't. It also operated under the broad assumption that Trump's voting bloc was impenetrable; hence, any third candidate would exclusively draw votes away from Biden. This assumption was undermined when polls indicated the third choice would draw evenly from both sides. I remained confident that it was impossible to determine who it might draw from until a ticket was named. I was even more confident that Biden would lose to Trump in the coming months.

I joined the group as their national director in spring 2023 and would have a front row seat to the left's attack on this group's constitutional rights, including access to the ballot. What started as jabs and attacks on television, email, print, and through surrogates soon expanded into something far more sinister.

During their ballot operation and movement to assemble a bipartisan ticket, No Labels allowed their website ownership to expire for a brief period, just long enough for an adversary to snatch it up. That organization then edited the content so it would appear No Labels was a pro-Trump organization. They placed many pictures of Trump on it, while keeping the colors and logo the same to make it appear it was the same No Labels website. In response, No Labels filed a lawsuit, secured a temporary injunction in federal court, which forced the group to return the website back to No Labels. Through the litigation process, the identities of groups and persons working to block No Labels from accessing the ballot in various states were uncovered. Their methods were exposed and, ironically, all these groups were left-leaning activists and advocacy groups whose mission was "saving democracy." It also exposed their methods at halting No Labels and tarnishing its reputation.

"Our main focus should be brand destruction, but, where possible, we also need to throw up any and all roadblocks to stop them from being successful at signature-gathering," Lucy Caldwell, one of the anti-No Labels strategists, wrote in an email that was produced during litigation. Signature gathering, whether it be for candidates or ballot initiatives, is considered core political speech in America and is protected under the First Amendment. This has been upheld in several U.S. Supreme

Court documents. Hard to imagine the groups and people hellbent on "saving democracy" would fail to realize that.

Their efforts went beyond that, though.

In the trove of documents turned over, personal and professional harassment were proposed by several people and groups. One suggested the hiring of clowns and musicians to hang outside the home of No Labels' CEO Nancy Jacobson and perform, starting at 6 a.m. to wake her and her neighbors. Jacobson endured relentless attacks as did her staff yet never wavered in her mission to provide Americans with another choice.

The same people lobbing personal attacks at No Labels and its staff were also attacking their constitutional right to access the ballot. I have endured my share of personal attacks as this vitriol has become commonplace in today's politics. But the blocking of voters' access to the ballot cuts to the core of Democratic principles.

No Labels pressed on despite fierce opposition. They continued to secure wins, either procedurally or in the courts, to have a line on the ballot for the upcoming presidential election. More of the left began to offer their opinion and eventually the top brass began to weigh in on the efforts by No Labels. Speaker Pelosi said, "I think that our democracy is at risk, and I think that No Labels is perilous to our democracy. I say that without any hesitation." Biden was eventually forced to comment on the effort, saying "It's going to help [Trump]."

No Labels ultimately secured access to the ballot in nineteen states. If the effort had continued, the group would have secured even more. Yet, the most important part of the whole operation was finding the correct candidate. Despite best efforts by the organization, it was unable to identify the right candidate with the courage that could deliver a decisive victory. No Labels was not interested in filling a ballot line just to do it. It knew of the solemn responsibility it had to not be a spoiler but to stay true to the original mission. It had pledged to only nominate someone if Americans wanted another choice and if they found a ticket that could win. Many were disappointed a ticket was not nominated by the group. But it takes courage for a credible candidate to shun their own party and place their country ahead of all else. And that hero never arrived.

The efforts by those on the left to undermine a constitutional right and deny Americans a choice they so desperately wanted will be impossible to forget. And the greatest hypocrisy of all: they were claiming Trump would be the death of democracy. It would have been a bad enough stain on the reputation of Democrats if their efforts had ceased there. But that was not the case.

Season Two of eroding democracy began on July 21, 2024, when Biden announced he would be ending his reelection campaign. The plan was put into overdrive to immediately replace him with Vice President Harris with not even a semblance of a primary election. Harris pollster Molly Murphy later described this transition. "There was a lot of operations on the legal side of calling delegates, on making sure she was on the path to become the nominee to avoid a competitive primary and open process," she said.

On the same day Biden ended his campaign, he endorsed his vice president, all but snuffing out a primary process. The Obamas followed five days after. Pretty soon, the writing was on the wall that Harris was the successor, and no voters would have the opportunity to change that. This coronation of Harris was Act 2 of Democrats' subversion of their voters' opportunity to choose.

We've all heard the saying, "It's the principle, not the money." Of course, in most times it is the money. But, in this case, it was both. It was about the principle. It was about the *Democratic* Party giving their voters a chance to participate in a *democratic* process. Allowing them the opportunity to vote on their nominee in a full, open and transparent process.

It was also about the money because Harris was not the best candidate.

The best predictor for future success is past success. While running for the nomination back in 2019, Harris consistently polled in single digits and eventually suspended her campaign before the first primary votes were taken. Reflect on that. Sitting here writing this, I secured as many delegates as Harris did in the 2019 Democratic primary for president and I didn't even run.

Although Biden placed her on the ticket with him, her poll numbers never meaningfully improved. After almost a year in office, in November 2021, her favorability rating was at 28 percent. Her image never noticeably improved. Just about a month before she ascended to be the presidential nominee, in late June 2024, about 63 percent of Americans had an unfavorable view of her. Months before Biden stepped down, amongst murmurs of nudging him to do so, there were also backroom conversations on how to instead replace her on the ticket with someone new with higher favorability ratings. The hope was a new vice president might give the Biden ticket a shot of adrenaline, enough to make it across the finish line.

Having witnessed Harris's underwhelming campaign in 2020 and knowing the favorability ratings while serving under Biden, Democrats put her forward with eyes wide open about how she was generally viewed by the public. So despite considering replacing her on the Biden ticket, they decided to elevate her to run as the Democratic "nominee" for president.

In the name of saving democracy, the Democratic Party subverted the democratic process, ignored the will of voters and coronated someone whose track record with voters and Americans was equally poor and well documented. Long after Harris was handed the nomination, Democrats continued to make "saving democracy" their theme even though they had so blatantly disregarded it. The polling continued to show that this message was not breaking through. Most likely because voters were not buying it. And they were not buying it because they did not trust the messenger. They rejected the ethos.

The best indicator for future performance is past performance. The same goes with ethos or credibility. If voters feel like they have been misled by a person or party, they are less likely to trust them in the future. Credibility matters. Ethos is important. When voters feel like a candidate or party is not being truthful with them on one matter, they are less likely to believe them on another. The more instances of betrayal or hypocrisy that stack up, the more their credibility crumbles.

That leads us to gerrymandering. It's a term that many Americans are not familiar with but is a core cause of the dysfunction you see in the U.S. House of Representatives. It is the process that allows partisan politicians to draw district boundaries and select their own voters as opposed to allowing voters to select their politicians. With Geographical Information Systems (GIS), voter data and computer systems, the drawing of a district boundary can be done with surgical precision on computer programs to ensure one party rule in those districts for years to come.

The practice creates a stark imbalance between the voters and their representation. For example, North Carolina can be viewed as a purple state in which one would expect a congressional delegation of half Democratic and half Republican. However, their gerrymandered maps are drawn with only just over 21 percent Democratic districts, despite Trump only winning 51 percent of the vote in 2020. In my home state of South Carolina, President Biden received over 43 percent of the vote in 2020 and VP Harris received just over 40 percent in 2024. Despite that level of participation for Democrats, they hold only one out of seven congressional districts, which accounts for 14 percent. How does a state that consistently votes for Democrats at a level of 40 percent hold just 14 percent of the Congressional seats? Gerrymandering is your answer.

For the past several years, voting rights have been the chant of the Democratic Party. Automatic voter registration. Banning straight ticket voting. Same day voter registration. And yes, banning gerrymandering was on that Christmas list as well.

Democrats have bannered the message that they, and only they, are the saviors of democracy. What has undermined that is they have been engaged in the same practices they openly criticize. In 2020, the partisan breakdown of the New York's congressional delegation was twenty Democrats and seven Republicans. Following the 2020 census, the Democratic legislature seized on the opportunity to redraw the maps and were able to squeeze out three more Democratic districts away from Republicans. New York's Supreme Court ultimately brought the hammer down on these illegally drawn districts and made an Independent Redistricting Commission (IRC) redraw the boundaries. Instead of giving Democrats three additional seats, the IRC took one away from them. Had the

Democrats tightened existing boundaries and kept a similar map, they might have retained their overall and healthy thirteen-seat advantage (or more). Instead, they reached too far. They were admonished by the New York Supreme Court and lost a Democratic district.

Democrats find a way to engage in the practice of gerrymandering even in states where they serve in the minority.

Following the 2020 census in South Carolina, Democratic Congressman Jim Clyburn coordinated with the state Republican Party to add even more Black voters (i.e. Democratic voters) to his district (even though he won in 2020 by over thirty-eight points) and move more Republican voters into the 1st Congressional District. At that time the 1st Congressional District was the only competitive district. I won it by one point in 2018 and then lost it by a point in 2020. Since then, no Democrat has come close. By moving more Republican voters into the district, Clyburn helped cannibalize the only competitive district to pad his own, already comfortable margin for victory.

In late 2021, many states were going through the legislative process of redrawing their maps. At this time, I testified in front of the South Carolina Senate subcommittee about the impacts of the proposed maps and what it meant for democracy. The next month, I launched an educational campaign to "Keep Charleston together" that helped educate my neighbors on how they were being moved into or out of different districts strictly for partisan gain. It was an issue I spoke about incessantly. It pained me to learn that not only was the sole Democratic congressman and my former colleague staying silent, but he was secretly working with the Republican party and against his own in the gerrymandering process.

Worse was this was not the first time Clyburn was involved

in the gerrymandering of South Carolina for his own gain and at the expense of Democrats. During the previous census back in 2010, it was reported his office was intimately involved in the gerrymandering process, even at times requesting certain businesses and homes be placed inside his own district boundary. I had heard this from various sources during my time serving with him and found it peculiar that he never spoke out publicly against gerrymandering even when the subject of voting rights was being discussed.

Unfortunately, he was not alone. Many Democrats across the country—members of Congress and members of state legislatures—engage in the practice to preserve their own political lives. In doing so, they place themselves first and their constituents last. Oftentimes, it leaves voters having no impact when they show up in November since the die is already cast on which party will prevail based upon the shape and makeup of the district.

Yes, Democrats do this. Yes, Republicans do this. Reapportionment (i.e. redistricting and, unfortunately, gerrymandering) happens every ten years following a census and in accordance with the U.S. Constitution.

However, in 2025 with the support of President Trump, Texas began redrawing its congressional map. The new lines would give Republicans five more seats, accounting for 79 percent of their congressional delegation, despite President Trump winning just 56 percent of the vote in the 2024 presidential election.

In response to the power grab by Texas Republicans, Democratic legislators fled the state to deny the body a quorum, hence preventing a vote on the new, gerrymandered map. Many fled to Illinois where its Governor JB Pritzker welcomed them with open arms, even calling them "heroes." Openly attacking Texas's gerrymandering directly opened up his state to criticism.

According to the Redistricting Report Card from RepresentUs and the Princeton Gerrymandering Project, Illinois was given an "F" for partisan fairness and for how badly counties were carved up. Its maps yielded 82 percent Democratic representation in a state where Democratic nominee and vice president received just 54 percent of the vote in the 2024 presidential election.

Asked pointedly on *Meet the Press* by host Kristen Welker, "What do you say to those who argue its hypocritical for you to criticize Texas for partisanship when your state also drew maps to boost your party's standing?" Governor Pritzker responded by attacking the process of Texas redistricting mid-decade and then pivoted to assaulting President Trump. The host went back to highlighting the hypocrisy by asking Governor Pritzker, "You talk about preserving democracy. How do you preserve democracy if you're using the same tactics you've criticized Texas Republicans for?" No meaningful answer followed by the Governor because not one existed.

Democratic states, including Illinois, New York, and California were quick to respond to Texas's gerrymandering efforts by threatening to do the same. California Governor Gavin Newsom said he would (and did) call for a special election in November 2025 to approve Proposition 50 entitled the "Election Rigging Response Act." Its purpose would be to bypass the state's independent redistricting commission, allow the state legislature to redraw its congressional maps that would give Democrats five more seats to offset the new Texas maps.

The political spats between red and blue states and gerrymandering are disappointing and fail to serve our country well. We all deserve better. Republicans share much of the blame. But since my focus within these pages is on what the Democratic Party can do to better its standing, and restore trust with voters,

I must point out the obvious. A governor who approved heavily gerrymandered maps has little credibility to attack another state at doing the same. Democrats cannot decry efforts done by the other side when they themselves have engaged in similar behavior. Attack or respond appropriately, but it is the demonstration of moral superiority by the Democratic Party that voters are clearly seeing. Implying "election rigging," when the Democratic Party does the same, comes off as hypocritical. A Party cannot hold itself out to be the one and only party "saving democracy" and at the same time engage in the very same practices it openly condemns.

If the Democratic Party is going to be aggressive and fight back, they need to simply tamp down (or cease) the moral righteousness, as people see through it as evidenced by Governor Pritzker's confrontation on *Meet the Press*. Otherwise, the trust of voters in the Democratic Party will continue to slip away.

What I have seen and heard leads me to believe much ground has been lost already.

"Why should I even bother voting? I feel like my vote doesn't even count," is what I would hear constantly while on the campaign trail in South Carolina. They had every reason to feel that way. In recent presidential elections, the state always goes for the Republican nominee. All congressional districts were but a lock for six Republicans and one Democrat. And they had only their politicians to blame for it. While both parties engage in it, only one party supposedly fights against it, which comes off as hypocritical.

The Democratic president, Woodrow Wilson, proclaimed that the world must be made safe for democracy. Instead, and to borrow from the words of the great North Carolina author Thomas Wolfe, Wilson's own Democratic Party is now "making the world safe for hypocrisy." We cannot close the discussion on the hypocrisy democracy without discussing pardons.

President Biden's son, Hunter, came under federal investigation for crimes related to taxes and possession of a firearm. In June 2024, Hunter was found guilty on the firearm charges and in September 2024 he pleaded guilty to the tax-related charges. The issue of whether President Biden would pardon his son became a popular question by reporters and a political liability for the Biden administration. Yet, in December 2023 and referring to Hunter, Biden stated, "I will not pardon him." In July 2024, White House press secretary, when asked if Biden would pardon his son, stated, "It's still a no. It will be a no." "No" was the consistent answer from Biden and his administration when asked about the possibility of pardoning his son.

But on December 1, 2024, President Biden did pardon his son.

I empathize with President Biden here. As a father and in a situation like his, I may have pardoned my son, too. I think most fathers would. If any father had the power to save their son, to spare them from sitting in a cold empty jail for similar crimes, they would likely take that opportunity. Most would not have lied about it. It is not the act of the pardon, but the commitment he made *not* to do it. Had he simply left it open, I do not believe it would have received as much political blowback.

When Trump was supposedly considering pardoning his own family members, many in the Democratic Party as well as the left-leaning media, pounced on it. President Biden said back in 2020 on CNN, "Well, it concerns me in terms of what kind of precedent it sets and how the rest of the world looks at us as a nation of laws and justice, you're not going to see in our administration, that kind of approach to pardons." Then

Senate Majority leader Chuck Schumer referred to President Trump's possible pardons for his family as "a gross abuse of the presidential pardon authority." Many more lobbed ferocious attacks against President Trump yet remained silent when the same actions were contemplated by President Biden.

Even after the 2024 presidential election, the Party continued to find ways to subvert democracy. In November 2025, Democratic Congressman Chuy Garcia from Illinois announced he would be retiring, citing health complications and other personal reasons. Congressman Garcia was a dedicated public servant, having been elected to office nearly forty years prior to his resignation from Congress. No doubt he had many accomplishments to be proud of. Yet, people mostly remember *how* you leave. On November 5, 2025, the last day to file paperwork for the Democratic primary, Congressman Garcia's chief of staff, Patty Garcia, filed her nominating petition to appear on the ballot. The next day, on November 6, 2025, Congressman Garcia withdrew his petition, leaving Patty Garcia as the sole Democrat (and imminent successor) to run for the seat. Any doubt that this might have been coincidence was quickly dispelled when it was uncovered the very first signature Patty Garcia collected was none other than the congressman himself. He inked his name on her petition two days before the filing deadline. It was a deceptive bait and switch that deprived 734,000 residents of Illinois's 4th Congressional District of their right to elect their own Representative. It is the epitome of election interference and the antithesis to protecting democracy.

Democrat Congresswoman Marie Gluesenkamp Perez was brave enough to express her disappointment in her colleague's actions and filed a privileged resolution condemning the same. In it, she called his maneuver "fundamentally undemocratic" for essentially "anointing an heir" by having his chief of staff, Patty Garcia, file just before the deadline." There were other Democrats who shared Congresswoman Perez's sentiment. However, the real disappointment came from those who rushed to defend his actions.

Jon Lovett, former speechwriter for President Obama, tweeted, "Should members of Congress play games with their retirement announcements in order to hand pick their successors instead of letting voters decide? No. But with democracy under threat, it is not the time to point this out." Mr. Lovett was not alone. Those who turn a blind eye to such undemocratic actions are wildly oblivious to the short-term and long-term impacts to what little trust the public held in the Party.

Worse, some allegedly cheered on the anti-democratic actions. Congresswoman Perez went on CNN and said, "Immediately after the news broke about how Chuy had basically chose his successor, I saw a lot of members congratulating him on how clever and slick it was." Such underhanded political maneuvers are not monopolized by Democrats. In April 2024, Republican Congressman Bill Posey abruptly announced he would not seek reelection. His hand-picked replacement, Florida State Senator Mike Haridopolos, had quietly entered the race shortly before Congressman Posey withdrew. These are the ugly sides of politics. The difference between these two occurrences is that Republicans do not wrap themselves up in the "Save Democracy" flag while campaigning. The Party cannot claim the moral high ground while turning a blind eye, or worse, supporting such actions that undermine our democracy. One has to change and I think we know which one that is.

Some may read the above and believe that placing a heavy hand on the nomination process, gerrymandering or politically motivated pardons are simply the parts of politics. This may be true, but it misses the point. George Bernard Shaw famously states, "Some men see things as they are and say 'why'? I dream of things that never were, and say 'why not?'" Can't we do better? Can't my beloved Democratic Party do better?

I wish to emphasize that when a Party holds itself out to be morally superior to another on certain issues—like upholding democracy—and then blatantly falls short, its credibility implodes. It drives a stake through the heart of ethos.

Once credibility is undermined in one area, it easily spreads to other areas. *If the Democratic Party is not being truthful on gerrymandering, how can I trust what it tells me about healthcare or education?* Albert Einstein famously said, "Whoever is careless with the truth in small matters cannot be trusted with important matters." I do not believe these are small matters. And that makes the issue of credibility more dire.

The words "credibility" and "respect" are closely related. If voters respect a candidate, it is likely because they find him credible. Respect is a two-lane highway, though. And if politicians are seeking it from voters, they must first give it.

6

THE CURRENCY OF RESPECT

Civility is the sum of all the virtues, and the parent of them all.
                                        – THEODORE ROOSEVELT

The 2018 mid-terms brought dozens of new candidates out of the woodwork, myself included.

Politics had always been in the back of my mind, probably because I grew up with a father who was a public servant. Bill Cunningham's service to our country started when he was drafted in the Vietnam war. He would serve in Vietnam, Korea, and Germany before returning back to western Kentucky to start a family. As a bonus, he also met his wife while stationed overseas. Their courtship began over a Memorial Day weekend when he and his colleagues took leave to explore an island off the coast of Italy. My mother, who was working overseas at the time, also chose Sardinia as her vacation spot and fate would handle the rest. Through an immeasurable amount of charm, humor, and idealism, my dad convinced her to move back to western Kentucky and make a life together. The rest was history.

Exposed to politics as a child, one thing stood out: how my father treated people. And as a result, how they treated him. It was not uncommon for people to approach him in the store and thank him for the way he had treated their son or daughter, even if it was when he was prosecuting them on behalf of the Commonwealth or sentencing them later in his career when he served on the bench. "Treat everyone with dignity and respect," he had told his sons. He would back it up with deeds.

When he became a judge, defendants would appear in front of him to enter a guilty plea. They'd raise their hand and affirm it was being done "freely and voluntarily." The optics of a person shackled and stating they were making decisions freely and voluntarily never sat well with him, so he would request the bailiff remove the handcuffs and ankle chains during the plea. While this request may have seemed symbolic more than anything else, the justice system is one he swore to protect, and any chipping away at its corners would not be allowed under his watch.

Every American has constitutional rights, and when they are applied unevenly, our system begins to erode. Racism in western Kentucky lurked just beneath the surface and, at times, on top. The county I grew up in was dry, prohibiting the sale of alcohol. But making something illegal doesn't make it extinct.

Most of the bootleggers were older African Americans and were quite popular with anyone who disliked driving forty miles to the nearest wet county. Inevitably, local police would arrest one of their customers—oftentimes a highschooler—and use them to set up and arrest the bootleggers. Wearing chains into court, they would stand in front of a judge to learn their fate.

Meanwhile, on the more prosperous side of town existed the Elks Club and any other club or establishment that sold plenty of alcohol and made little noise. Fed up with the blatant and racial discrimination, my father lectured the police to not arrest and bring any more Black men in front of him until they started hauling the white ones out of the country clubs. In a time and place like the 1980s in the rural South, this viewpoint was uncommon and unpopular. Yet, my father had grown up witnessing the racial disparities that engulfed his generation and was trying his best to correct them, however small or large.

He is who he is because of how he was raised. And where he was raised.

I asked an old high school friend, "What do you think the biggest benefit was growing up in a small town?"

"You had to learn to get along with people," he said without hesitation.

Kuttawa, an Indian name for "Village in the Woods," had roughly 550 people within her borders. Lyon County, which contained Kuttawa, had a bit over eight thousand. When you are forced to see people again day in and day out, treating them like anything less than human is just not an option if you wish to live a good life.

Growing up in a small town in the rural south, respect was the legal tender. In the democracy of the barber shop, the barefoot urchin had his hair cut before the bank president simply because the little sprite was there first. The most successful farmer in the county has coffee with the town's inebriate, simply because they've been friends all their lives. The county chairman for the Republican Party and the chairman of the Democratic Party would take up offering together on Sunday morning. The prosecuting attorney and defense attorney would have breakfast together before heading to the courthouse where they would engage in verbal combat. A deal where a local mechanic agrees to fix your car for a certain amount is not even sealed with a handshake. His word is enough. Mutual respect and common sense. That's what I grew up with. That is who I am. My dad knew it. I learned it. I wish so many others had as well.

My "why" did have a Trump element. I did not care for the way he spoke to or of others. I did not want that to be the norm. Despite how toxic politics was becoming, there was something noble—in my mind and from my exposure to it—in public service. It was enough to push me off the sidelines.

So in June 2017 after weeks and weeks of meetings and receiving opinions and feedback—some solicited, some not—I declared my candidacy for Congress. Along with that announcement was another: "The Democratic Party needs new leadership now. If elected, I will not vote for Nancy Pelosi for Speaker. Time to move forward and win again." If my announcement for Congress was an explosion, then that tweet was the match. It immediately hurled a no-name young attorney into national headlines, becoming the first Democrat to make such a pledge.

It would not be the last time I publicly challenged leadership within my own party. But tone matters. I felt it was important to do so in a non-disparaging manner. There are always ways to disagree without being disagreeable. Science validates the importance of *how* something is said compared to *what* is said.

Dr. Mehrabian was an American psychologist best known for his pioneering research on non-verbal communication. He came up with the 7–38–55 rule, which states that when a message is received by a person, 7 percent is verbal, 38 percent is vocal, and 55 percent is visual. No one understands this better than Winston Churchill who said, "Tact is the ability to tell a person to go to hell in such a way where they look forward to the trip."

Most assume that in order to win—in a courtroom, at the ballot office, or wherever—you must denigrate your opponent at every turn. Because of this, it has become exhausting to live on planet Earth. Yes, there are times to stand your ground, to advocate for your position passionately. Despite what appears on the news or how social medial algorithms are programmed, I believe the world is begging for something else. Americans would love to see any small courtesy extended to the other side—however small—to give folks a short breath of hope and to reaffirm that there is a human side to this system that has become so inhumane. Treating people with dignity and respect.

My first real opportunity to do this in the political arena arrived in 2018.

When I launched my campaign, I assumed—as did virtually everyone—that I would be going up against former Governor Mark Sanford in the general election. All of us were wrong.

Every Republican during Trump's presidency was trying to find their footing those first two years (2016–2018). No one knew how to handle the daily questions of "Do you agree with the president when he said…" or "What do you have to say to …". Most were doing whatever it took to retain their seat and navigate the political waters safely. Sanford simply said what was on his mind, with the good ole fashioned, "Well, I would respectfully disagree with the President on …". Notwithstanding the fact that Sanford's voting record with President Trump was near perfect, the President still took aim at him. He would become the first political casualty in the Trump era, losing his job simply for the sake of an honest disagreement. When the votes were called for the Republican primary, Sanford just barely fell short.

So what does this have to do with treating people with respect?

Weeks after Katie Arrington pulled off this monumental upset against Mark Sanford, she was involved in a horrific car crash, sending her to the hospital where she would remain for weeks. At the time of the accident, we were not sure if she would survive. I first learned about it when Tyler Jones, my general consultant, woke me up at 5 a.m. the next morning to inform me of the accident.

With little discussion, I decided we should temporarily suspend the campaign. Nothing felt good about continuing to campaign as normal while someone's life hung in the balance. I tried to put myself in the shoes of her family and we simply wanted to eliminate anything that might distract from that which was most important: her health and safety. Politics could wait.

In making this decision, there was no blueprint. If you google "my opponent is in a car wreck, what should I do with my campaign?" your query would come up empty. But when you stop thinking like a politician and just ask yourself what's the right thing to do, the answer becomes pretty obvious.

Vice President Mike Pence agreed. As did many others on the Republican side who may have disagreed with me on substance, but have made comments to me privately and publicly how that moment stood out in a political season that was rife with rancor.

This lesson obviously extends beyond politics.

Many years ago, I had lost a case to a seasoned attorney in Charleston where the court even ordered my client to pay attorneys' fees for the other side. After the matter had concluded, I got a handwritten note from the opposing counsel saying what a pleasure it was having us on the other side. Genuine and simple. And I never forgot it. I know there are many attorneys who make a very good living steamrolling people with little to no regard for human emotion. However, by far the most successful and respectful practitioners follow the same approach as the one I mentioned.

The way I treated others who I disagreed with ultimately got me elected to Congress. And when I was there, I saw no reason to change.

As a congressman, I remember the attendance at my first town hall was a mixed bag. The crowd mirrored the district, which, unfortunately for me, meant there were more who disagreed with me than agreed. I arrived a half hour early to greet everyone as they entered. A handshake and short hello to hopefully defuse the situation. I found folks were more likely to say disparaging or negative comments about people they did not know or were not geographically close to. For example, think about all the keyboard warriors out there. A person is more likely to spew toxic words against someone they only know through their television set or computer than they are about a neighbor or a local commissioner they would see at the youth baseball league or grocery store. I did town halls because I wanted people to feel like they were being heard and treated with respect.

I would routinely look for ways to put that respect on display, from the start to finish. Every town hall would open with the pledge of allegiance, and I would select one person from the crowd to lead us in it. Front row, MAGA hat, red shirt, or any clothing that told me they were not likely to be there to pat me on my back made them a prime candidate from my vantage point. It was a simple gesture that caught people off-guard every time, showed them we were all alike and hopefully lower the temperature of the discussion that followed.

"It's easy to be a sunny day Christian," my dad said. Forgiving people is hard, especially those who seek to ruin you. Until you have enemies—and political enemies are only one breed, but a special breed—I'm not sure you fully appreciate how difficult it is to treat everyone the same: with dignity and respect. I have fallen short and will continue to fall short at times. Fortunately, God judges on effort and not results.

In Congress, the people and groups that aim to test your values are in ample supply. There are some whose jobs are simply to needle you, hurling questions and insults at you simply to elicit a reaction.

Trackers are entry-level jobs for any young man or woman who wishes to work in politics. They're called that because they track where you go and are constantly filming you and asking questions intended to get under your skin. What they want is a reaction; they are not concerned with your answer. Just a few seconds of you flying off the handle at them or saying something that can be clipped and taken out of context and then run on TV at high levels to dissuade your electorate.

Many trackers have no boundaries. My friend, Senator Andy

Kim of New Jersey, told me one tracker had followed him to his kid's daycare center. How to respond to trackers is limited. You can fly off the handle, try to engage and persuade, or simply ignore them. The latter is the best bet.

I had to deal with trackers constantly, in Washington DC and back at home. I got used to it and would often acknowledge their presence in a respectful tone and then move on. I got to know one of my trackers in South Carolina. Tyler was hired by the National Republican party to follow me around during the 2020 reelection campaign. He would open his tripod and set up his camera at every event and when I was walking out, he would break it down and leave. He would make fleeting comments to me as the election neared, making it clear he agreed with a lot of what I said and this was just a job for him and he needed the money. The last time I saw him he extended his hand to shake and told me quietly he was voting for me.

How we treat others in moments of disagreement is telling—and indicative of the respect we earn.

In December 2019, New Jersey Congressman Jeff Van Drew made the decision to switch parties from Democratic to Republican. It took the entire caucus by surprise and not even a member from the New Jersey delegation was given a heads up. Right after the news broke, I was in the cloak room. This is the sort of the locker room for members of Congress and it is attached to the House floor. There is a Democratic one and Republican one, attached to but located off their respective sides of the House floor. It's a place with couches, old school phone booths (members can close them and have private conversations), and chairs for members to relax in, shoot the bull, and watch TV. On this day when Van Drew had made the switch, Democratic members were crammed in the cloak room huddled around the TV that was broadcasting him in the Oval Office with Trump, sitting in those side by side chairs while the President was shoveling praise upon Van Drew for being so courageous.

We all watched in silence and then one by one each member peeled themselves away, often uttering obscenities in our colleague's direction. Van Drew's staff quit en masse. I can only imagine the emails his office received from constituents, donors, and political groups.

No punches were pulled in the press either. When asked about the news, Democratic Congressman Tom Malinowski, a fellow New Jerseyan, said, "It's pretty inconsequential, I think, given how inconsequential he was in this place."

Jeff had always been incredibly respectful and polite since he arrived in DC and, in my opinion, deserved the same in return. So when asked by the press, I responded, "Jeff's a good friend of mine as a Democrat, and Jeff's going to be a good friend of mine as a Republican, too."

A politician switching parties is not entirely rare.

Years later, a friend of mine who had served as a Democratic solicitor in South Carolina for several years decided to switch parties and run as a Republican for Attorney General. He cited numerous alleged defects of the Democratic Party following the disastrous election cycle of 2024. However, the reality was that running statewide in South Carolina as anything other than a Republican was an exercise in futility. Afterall, South Carolina is one of a few states that has "straight ticket voting" whereby the first question on the ballot asks the voter if they want to vote all Democratic or all Republican. And with the click of a bubble, their entire ballot is populated accordingly, and they are out of the voting booth in two minutes no matter the number of offices up for election.

Back to my solicitor friend, David Pascoe. Upon his announcement of switching parties, the Chair of the South Carolina Democratic Party gave this scathing public response:

> Who are you fooling, David? Do you think South Carolina Republicans are going to let a twenty-year Democratic solicitor who suddenly has a change of heart be their nominee for attorney general? We trust his new political home will embrace his long-held Democratic values with the same enthusiasm—or at the very least, google them. When the South Carolina GOP primary voters reject you in 2026, don't expect the voters in Calhoun, Dorchester, and Orangeburg to allow you to keep your job.

Politics is rough. Yet, the above was completely unnecessary. The Chair could have put in a comment about David's service to law and order, the Democratic Party or even just offering himself up for public service. But our current political ecosphere affords no room for cordiality or respect, even when it is most needed.

It's almost as if this behavior is expected in this line of work. At the very least, it is encouraged. Leadership in both parties will place pressure on members to wallow in the partisan muck for fear that any polite overture could tilt the balance in the opposing party's favor.

Congressman Garrett Graves was a Republican from Louisiana with whom I had staunch disagreements over off-shore oil drilling, debating him on and off the House floor on several occasions. Despite these differences, I tried to seek out other pieces of legislation on which we could work together. The benefit to him was that my party was in the majority and, hence, could move bills through, and me, being one of the most vulnerable members on the left side of the aisle, was someone Democratic leadership wanted to help. The bad side for him is that he would be working with a Democrat.

While exercising in the House gym one day, Graves did tell me that he would continue working with me on several bills, but informed me that he had been warned, by leadership, not to for fear that it could benefit me politically. Garrett was a member who liked to get things done and someone who placed effectiveness over politics any day. There were many issues we worked on through the Natural Resources Committee on which we both served. It was a stark reminder that most in Washington DC would rather have the country and their constituents suffer if it meant they or their party could benefit politically from short-sighted tactics like the above. One of the largest miscalculations made in politics is the assumption that being cordial is a weakness, when, in reality, it is just the opposite.

Small gestures can have big impacts. Even something as minor as a phone can tell you all you need to know about a person.

Back in 2017, I was in Mayor Joe Riley's office in downtown Charleston discussing my longshot bid to unseat Mark Sanford. The mayor was one of the most effective mayors in the history of Charleston and considered to be the gold standard for executives wanting to run a city. He was also a masterful politician, retaining his title as mayor for forty years and transforming Charleston from an unimpressive town to a shining economic and tourism beacon. I had met him back in 2001 when I was attending college and my dad, then a circuit court judge, had written him requesting him to meet with me.

Fast forward to that day in early 2017 and I'm sitting in his office asking for his formal endorsement. Standing at his desk, he picks up his phone, dials a number, and when the person on the other end of the line answers, he says, "Congressman, I just want to let you know that I'll be endorsing Joe Cunningham in his run for Congress. His family and mine are good friends and I'll be throwing my support behind him. I just wanted to let you know."

I could not hear what Mark Sanford had said but am fairly certain he was not the least bit concerned about a Democrat, with no name ID and no money, coming at him in his safe and gerrymandered seat. But it was the simple act of making the phone call that stuck with me. The Mayor had the class to give Sanford a heads up and have him hear it from him directly. It was a courtesy that has, unfortunately, become increasingly rare in today's politics.

While running in the Democratic primary for governor of South Carolina in 2022, I had former supporters who endorsed one of my primary opponents. That is to be expected. Any pain or disappointment that naturally flows from these instances could have easily been blunted by a simple phone call. A heads up. Unfortunately, however, gestures like the one the Mayor had made are disappearing from politics. And with it, decency as well.

The world can be unforgiving and I don't intend to give the impression that the golden rule is enough to carry the day, every day. But it's a start. A foundation to build upon. In today's political environment with the nonstop barrage of insults and putdowns, small acts or words shine through. And they can afford politicians the ability to stand out from a crowd while offering the public a breath of fresh air so desperately needed. Lady Mary Wortley Montagu put it more simply when she said, "Civility costs nothing, and buys everything."

Respect is the key that unlocks the door to constructive dialogue. It cannot be demanded; it must be earned. And once earned, communication becomes far easier. If the Democratic Party wants to win back voters, it must start by earning their respect—and then focus on how it speaks to them.

7

MEET THEM WHERE THEY ARE

Words are, of course, the most powerful drug used by mankind.
—RUDYARD KIPLING

The Castle is what they call it. A massive fortress-like structure puzzled together from couch-sized blocks of old limestone. It stands on the edge of the Cumberland River in western Kentucky. Nearly 140 years old, it is the state's only maximum-security prison and sits in the county where I grew up. My father had the good fortune of being born one hundred yards outside the prison walls and grew up with its larger-than-life presence hovering in the background. Later, while serving as a judge, he would preside over cases brought by inmates, including criminal activity and alleged violations of their civil rights. He would frequently walk the prison yard with the warden, who kept the pulse on the prison community and maintained order amongst a most unorderly crowd.

One day when he and my dad were walking the yard, an inmate who was standing on a low wall just above them, engaged in conversation.

"Hey, Warden. I got a question for ya!" he started.

Before he could continue, the warden firmly and respectfully told him to come down off the wall and present himself eye to eye. In the warden's mind, there were two reasons behind the command. First, for security purposes, after all, they were among maximum security inmates that included mass murderers, rapists, and kidnappers. Never yield the high ground to any person who might intend to harm you. Another reason was respect. Don't be talking down to the warden. And the warden will not talk down to you. On a yard with hardened criminals, mutual respect still exists.

It was the warden's reflex to reply, "Come down here and talk," because he understood the value of speaking to someone on their level.

Sometimes you must go *up* to someone's level to communicate and other times you have to go *down*. An airline stewardess told me that during her training, they instructed her to squat down when speaking with passengers. To come down to their level and meet them eye to eye when talking with them as opposed to simply hovering over them and talking down to them. She told me it makes the passengers feel more respected and heard and lends itself to a better encounter. And even if the customer is rude or makes a request that is unreasonable or cannot be fulfilled, they at least feel heard.

Just as important as the level of communication are the words being used to communicate. This is an area where Democrats fail miserably at connecting with everyday voters. They invent words that are unnecessary like: "sustainability," "cisgender," and "food insecurity." The average American does not speak in these terms, so why would Democrats believe these are the best words in which to connect with the common voter? Most Americans do not know what *binary* or *non-binary* is. Nor could they describe what each letter in LGBTQIA+ means. No one I know who immigrated from South or Central America has asked to be referred to as *Latinx*. The public's lack of understanding of these terms is exceeded only by their lack of desire to learn them.

But it's not just the superfluous (get it?) words Democrats throw around, it's the jumble of words Democrats put together. A social media post in December 2024 by the White House touted launching the "first-ever National Strategy to Counter Islamophobia and Anti-Arab Hate." Not exactly the headline that simply rolls off the tongue.

Within the "strategy" of this plan, it "sets forth a whole-of-government and whole-of-society effort to combat these forms of discrimination." What does that even mean? And who is this message or "strategy" intended to reach? Yes, Islamophobia and other forms of hate are real and should be addressed. If the White House is attempting to solve this problem, its solutions should be tangible otherwise it could come off as incoherent at best and virtue signaling at worst.

I cannot tell you the reason the above wording was employed. Perhaps the belief is if the words describing an idea are sophisticated, so is the idea. But these phrases sound like they were manufactured in an academic institution to impress professors or grad students, not everyday Americans. It can come off as an attempt to wrap a poorly hatched idea in a shiny box with a fancy bow.

Following the raging wildfires in California in January 2025, which devastated over 57,000 acres and took the lives of at least twenty-nine individuals, former Vice President Harris toured the scorched ground. "We must as a society and a country invest in adaptation and resilience," she said. "We have to understand these extreme weather occurrences are extreme, but they are increasingly less rare." Perhaps it was not one of her better soundbites, but it was clipped and circulated, and critics posed the questions of how to "invest in adaptation" or highlight that "extreme weather occurrences are extreme."

Word salads like this also continue to undermine what remaining trust Americans have in Democrats. If I don't understand how the "whole of government" plan or the "environmental sustainability" policy affects me, why would I trust the prescription or tax plan you put out next week? If a voter feels like you're speaking above them or trying to pull one over on them, they are less likely to trust you in the weeks to come.

Equally important as credibility is the public's understanding. Democrats, more than Republicans, feel the need to answer every single nuance even if they tie themselves up in the explanation. There is a saying that if you cannot explain it to a six-year-old, it's too complicated. Republicans have known this for quite some time. *Build the wall. No men in women's sports. Cut taxes.* Whether or not you agree with any of these policies, you understand what's being said.

Furthermore, the liberal wing of our party needs to learn the wisdom of saying nothing when nothing needs to said. This is especially true of those who hold national office or wish to influence those who do. The state of Wyoming is plenty capable of taking care of a controversial issue in a local school board race there. We need to learn to say, "None of our business." We often "lead with our chin" where we don't need to be and suffer some political damage in the process.

Just as important as what is said (or not said) is *where* it is said.

There was a younger man walking in circles on the side of a street underneath a lamppost. An older gentleman watched from afar for a few minutes, seeing the younger man pace back and forth, back and forth over the same area. After a while, the older gentleman came over and asked the younger man, "What are you looking for?"

"I lost my keys and am trying to find them."

"Where do you think you lost them?"

"A few hundred feet down that alley there," the young man said while pointing.

"So why are you looking around here?"

"Well, this is where the light is." The young man replied.

The story illustrates you can be doing the right thing, just in the wrong place. Location matters as much as the words and timing. Democrats can be spot on with their message, yet it fails to hit because it is not being delivered through the right medium or at the correct location. They will look for their keys under the light when they were lost in the dark.

In simplest terms, go where the people are! Do not let comfort or convenience dictate your actions. Otherwise, your message falls on deaf ears.

Fox News is the number one news station. Not many people understand how far ahead they are of their competitors like

CNN or, to a lesser extent, MS NOW. During the last week of November 2024, Fox News had an average of 1.4 million total viewers per day compared to 268,000 for CNN. Fox had over five times the number of viewers as CNN. They don't just simply outperform CNN or other networks; they dominate. Yet, you would be hard pressed to find a Democrat darken the doorsteps of their station.

Despite the breadth of the network's reach, most Democrats fear a Fox News camera worse than the devil fears holy water. During the tail end of the 2024 campaign, Secretary of Transportation Pete Buttigieg would appear on Fox News and become a very effective messenger for his party. Some other national Democrats would follow suit, but it was too little too late.

Whether out of fear of unfriendly questions, or on "principle," Democrats miss an incredible opportunity to speak directly to millions of Americans by turning down opportunities to appear on Fox or other conservative outlets.

Joe Rogan is another example. In late October 2024, Donald Trump went on Joe Rogan's podcast and within three days amassed over thirty-eight million views. Incredible! As many people are seeking their news and information outside of traditional media outlets, personalities like Joe Rogan have become increasingly popular and the numbers from Trump's interview are proof of that. And after Trump appeared on his show and enjoyed much success, Kamala Harris was afforded the same opportunity. She declined.

What a missed opportunity! Consider these facts. Joe Rogan's audience is between 70 and 80 percent male, is majority white, and falls within the 18–34 age range. At the same time Harris was polling eleven points behind Trump and earning just 42 percent support of men. So she had an opportunity to go on a show and speak directly to a massive audience of the same demographics for which she was underperforming. While an appearance on Joe Rogan's podcast would not have saved her campaign, it was an easy (and free) way to connect with voters she desperately needed. But instead of going to where those white male voters were, she kept searching for them under the streetlight.

Why would someone decline an interview that could be incredibly helpful? Her campaign said that some of her progressive staff was pushing back because Joe Rogan was viewed as more conservative, controversial and not a "friendly" host. Rogan had said that Harris wanted to avoid talking about controversial topics like marijuana legalization. It appears the progressive staff of Harris did not personally like Rogan and felt talking about weed was too risqué.

Media appearances are always a calculated decision if the reward outweighs the risk. This is often measured against the backdrop of whether you are behind or ahead. Declining opportunities like Fox or Rogan might have been prudent if Harris had a commanding lead. But she didn't, and all accounts suggest her campaign knew the same.

There are many reasons why Harris lost to Trump. This decision alone did not cost her the election. The strategy of avoiding uncomfortable questions asked in front of millions of voters failed Harris and the Democratic Party. Retreating to the comfort of CNN or MS NOW is not a winning strategy. If Democrats fail to snatch up these media opportunities, they will continue to struggle competing across the country in areas that have grass.

Now contrast that with how Trump handled an interview that his advisors most likely anticipated to be hostile or uncomfortable.

The National Association of Black Journalists (NABJ) extended invitations to both Trump and Harris to address their members following their convention. Harris initially declined but after Trump accepted the invitation, she agreed to the interview. I doubt anyone on Trump's team considered this to be a softball interview, considering his struggles within the African American community coupled with his past comments and actions that many viewed as racially insensitive. His interview was not without controversy and many of his comments made headlines and remained in the news long after the interview ended. But Trump showed up and spoke to a demographic with which he historically performed poorly to gain more ground.

Did it work? Depends on how you view it. In 2024, Trump won two out of ten Black voters, compared to just one out of ten the previous election cycle. With young Black men, Trump doubled his support in 2024 compared to 2020. Was it the interview with the NABJ that led to this improvement? Unlikely. But it was certainly the approach of showing up time and time again in the face of hostile hosts or questions.

While Harris may have understood politics, Trump understood the press. As a public figure for most of his life, Trump understood the value of press, even if, at times, it is bad press. At the least, it shows people you are not afraid to speak with them and face the fire.

Voters must see you, especially if they are already skeptical of you. It is not enough for Harris to simply form "White Men for Harris" groups and call it a day. Or print camo hats or masculine merchandise to give the appearance she appeals to people she does not. Voters can see through this and they did.

There is no substitution for showing up and being seen. Not just for the media interviews, but at normal events where real people go. Trump understood this and was routinely seen at UFC fights, football games and other sporting events. The benefits of attending large events such as these are endless. One, you have a large, captivated audience that sees your face and hears your name. It is immediate advertising and better than any thirty-second commercial you can buy. You remain in their minds long after the event ends. It also humanizes a candidate. People who like baseball want to vote for a candidate who likes to watch baseball, too. They desire a connection that makes them feel like the person they are voting for is not all that different from them. If a voter enjoys watching UFC fights, they'd prefer their presidential candidate also enjoy the same. And if they can enjoy those same things together, then all the better. It may not be a required box to check off or enough to overcome other qualities, but it certainly helps. It is a bond or connection that whispers into the voter's ear, "They're just like me."

In 2018, I launched a brewery tour in South Carolina's 1st Congressional District. No one had ever done it. Small breweries were popping up all over the state and the country, becoming more popular and providing a kid-friendly (and dog-friendly) atmosphere where families could relax. During that longshot race, we were incessantly looking for outside the box ideas on ways to connect with voters. And if they cost nothing, even better. I intended to visit every brewery within my congressional district. It was tricky considering how gerrymandered my district was. There would be many breweries that would have attracted voters but simply fell outside the district boundary because partisans had carved neighborhoods in or out based upon political leanings (and race).

We experienced a decent showing at the first few breweries we went to, especially for this Democrat with no name ID in a district virtually impossible to win. But at each brewery, I made a point to talk to nearly everybody in the brewery. In the early days, it was not that great a challenge considering the small number of attendees.

Oftentimes, unsuspecting patrons who had stopped in for a cold one on their way home from work would get caught up in the political dragnet, but they would go home at least knowing who their congressional candidate was. Or when an ad would come on their TV later, they could say, "I met that guy."

The most frequent comment I heard from folks was, "Man, you just don't see any politicians relaxing and having a beer with people." There was a sense of normalcy my presence in a local brewery brought to voters. Seeing a politician or candidate out of context was shocking. When they're used to seeing them in commercials or interviews on their television, it was refreshing to see them at a table on the other side of a restaurant or bar.

It adds credence to what is called the *beer test*. If you haven't heard the adage of the *beer test* it's this: the person who wins an election is the same person you'd prefer to have a beer with. Think back on the presidential elections of your lifetime and ask yourself, between the two candidates, who would you rather have a beer with? More often than not, that person you choose likely won the election. Being in a brewery and having a beer with voters effectively reverse engineered this litmus test and would hopefully give me an edge come election day. Or one could hope.

Retail politics is the original name for this, and despite the advancements in voter identification, polling and targeting, there's still nothing that can replace it. Voters will always sniff out what's real.

The Harris campaign adopted another strategy that focused on the masses and ended up being a mile wide and an inch deep.

A cornerstone of the Harris presidential campaign were large, impersonal concerts or rallies with celebrities, many of whom were paid for their support. News reports suggest the Harris campaign paid Oprah one million dollars for her nod of support for Harris, and Beyoncé was paid $165,000. The Democratic nominee collected many star-studded endorsements, which her campaign placed front and center. What they obviously missed was the lack of connection between the voters and endorsees. Why would such endorsements matter if voters did not feel those making the endorsement could sympathize with their daily plight? What did voters have in common with billionaires, entertainers, or the top 1 percent? Not much. So how much influence did these endorsements wield? Not much.

By placing an enormous amount of focus on these endorsements, the Harris campaign continued to turn off moderate voters and even many Democrats. When the campaign had ended and it was discovered how much money was paid out in exchange for these endorsements, it was a further insult to both the Harris supporters and those she was attempting to court.

Someone who had fundraised for Harris told me after the campaign, "I took four days of my vacation time to help plan and coordinate fundraisers for her. It pisses me off to find out this is how the money was spent." I will concede that the Harris campaign was not given much of a runway leading up to the election. That part was not their fault. How they used that runway to communicate with voters was.

Just as important as meeting voters where they are is *how* we talk to them. Talking *to* them, not *at* them.

The Democratic Party, for years, has correctly earned its reputation of being the party of elites. I heard this when I served in Congress. I brushed it off as applying only to the politicians from the big cities, but not me. Not for my other friends, who were elected by the suburban vote and had won districts in 2018 that went for Trump in 2016. But as time passed, I had a harder time justifying words and actions from my colleagues as well as the left-leaning media. The condescending tone of the Democratic Party went from conspicuous to apparent to obvious in a very short period.

I'm not sure if it became worse over the last few years or if it has always been this bad and I just failed to notice. I've asked similar questions several times to friends: "Does it seem that politics has become worse over the last few years or is it me?" I desperately want it to be the latter. I want to believe that it had not been so bad when I was in Congress. Or had it been this bad all along? Like many things in life, the answer is probably a little bit of both. Perhaps it is getting worse and I'm becoming more attune to it.

But as it relates to tone and respect, most people feel it has worsened. The national narrative against Democrats is that they are condescending. Many feel those in the Party, especially political leaders, are talking down to them, even when attempting to win their support. Insulting classes of people is a surefire way to ensure they vote against you. And once that starts, it's nearly impossible to bring them back.

No group of voters experience this condescending tone than those who live in rural areas and watch cable news. As a lifelong Democrat from a small town, it has been equally insulting and hurtful to witness my Party poke their finger in the eye of those who do not live in major cities. I sense the pain that rural voters feel when left wing cable news or Democrats lob insults at those who chose to live in towns without subways or sky-scrapers. Many within my Party could never believe that those who do not reside within walking distance of a Whole Foods do so willingly. Most remarks or swipes at rural voters may not be made intentionally. Some are made out of ignorance. Yet, they hit just the same. Those on the receiving end still endure the barb and are left with the sentiment that Democrats think they are better because of where they live.

Many of these slights, unfortunately, are done in a subtle manner. But the impact is immense. Back in early December 2023, in what seems like a lifetime ago, the obsession *de jour* was Hunter Biden and what crimes he may have committed. On the decision desk in Congress was whether to open an impeachment inquiry and at the center of said controversy was Republican Chairman of the House Oversight Committee, Rep. Jamie Comer. On Fox News, Comer was asked whether he had the votes to open an impeachment inquiry. Comer suggested that many moderate Republicans were on the fence, but that had shifted after they went back to their respective districts over Thanksgiving and heard firsthand from their constituents.

Comer said, "[The members] met people in Walmart, and people on Main Street, and they're like, 'What in the world have the Bidens done to receive millions and millions of dollars from our enemies around the world, and did they not pay taxes on it?'" He went on, "So they heard from their constituents: 'Yes, we want you to move forward. We want to know the truth, and we expect the Bidens to be held accountable for public corruption.'"

How did the left respond to Comer's comment about his colleagues meeting and listening to the "Walmart crowd"?

Ian Sams, a White House spokesman for oversight and investigations and special assistant to Biden, tweeted "Burisma, it's the talk of Walmarts nationwide!!!" he snarked with a laughing-cry-face emoji. Burisma was the Ukrainian energy company, whose board Hunter Biden sat on, which prompted speculation of corruption.

A HuffPost headline read "James Comer makes Walmart Comment That Draws Snickers From White House Spox." Cable news' response was similar.

There are a few interpretations to take from these elitist reactions, none of which benefit Democrats. The first being whoever shops at a Walmart are uneducated, lower-class, and their opinions on federal issues should matter very little, if at all. Another interpretation would be "Why are you even talking to people at Walmart? You should go to at least a Trader Joe's or Target to find someone with some sense." While many in the news or on Twitter (now X) did not directly say these things, it was implied. And whether you are insulting someone to their face or behind their back, it still hits the same.

This is why these small jabs matter. My parents shop at Walmart. In fact, they buy their produce there because the grocery store that was in our small hometown shuttered its doors thirty years ago. The most practical option for groceries and convenience is a super Walmart fourteen miles away from their home. Ironically, they live in Jamie Comer's district. So when folks "snicker" or "roll their eyes" about Walmart or its patrons, it says more about them than about the people who darken the doors of Sam Walton's establishments.

This was a passing comment by Comer. It did not make news for more than a few hours and it's unlikely many remember it. But it stood out to me because I was opening my eyes up to how poorly the liberal media and national Democrats spoke to rural voters. Was it getting worse or had this been the tone all along? Whatever the answer, I was noticing it more and more.

These may seem like small blips or sound bites. But just as

each note holds a space in a musical piece, all these comments and headlines form a melody that causes rural voters to turn away from the Democratic Party.

Another example of this had to do with the issue of border security. In early March 2024, an MSNBC panel was discussing a poll and on what issues people were voting. Specifically, they mocked voters after uncovering that those who lived in non-border states had concerns about the border and national security.

"And if you look at some of these exit polls, I live in Virginia," Jen Psaki started. "Immigration was the number one issue."

"Well, Virginia does have border with West Virginia," Rachel Maddow chimed in sarcastically. The panel enjoyed a good laugh and then moved on.

It was a totally unnecessary and snobbish poke at the good people of West Virginia. And we wonder why states like West Virginia have gone from a Democratic stronghold to solid Republican.

It was a run of the mill panel with the same liberal talking heads and a very ordinary comment to be coming from the same. Yet, it spoke volumes. The takeaway from anyone who might have been listening but not agreeing was, "No one should be concerned about border security unless you live in a state that shares a border with Mexico." Or "You don't even know what you should be worried about. Listen, we will tell you what to worry about and what not to worry about." The panel and its members could not fathom why Americans would be concerned about such an issue. In fact, their disbelief turned into ridicule.

While the media shares much of the blame, Democrats' surrogates do more than their fair share of damage. Back in early April 2024, Hillary Clinton sat down with Jimmy Fallon to discuss Americans' current two options for President. At that time, the vast majority of Americans were already exhausted with the Biden-Trump campaign and desperately wanted other options as opposed to a rematch of 2020.

"It's Biden versus Trump. Ok. We know that. What do you say to voters who feel upset that those are the two choices?" Jimmy Fallon asked Clinton.

"Get over yourself. Those are the two choices." Clinton responded.

Right out of the gate, it was a turnoff. There was no empathy for Americans' frustration with the candidates. There was no justification for Biden running for reelection even though he said he would not. No reason we were preventing a new generation of leadership to emerge. Her tone and words were more like a teacher talking to second graders than a world leader speaking to adults. Unfortunately, the condescending and insulting nature was right on brand for Clinton. And it didn't end there.

Hillary then continued to make the comparison between the two, stating the similarities (i.e., old age) as well as their contrast (criminal indictments).

"I don't understand why this is a hard choice," she continued. "But we have to go through an election…" as she shrugged. The demeanor and tone were akin to "This is how I feel and I'm right, but I guess we have to actually wait until voters cast their opinions."

In essence, it was America she did not understand, not "why this was a hard choice."

Some liberal outlets like *The View* amplified her comments and dissected them. Others associated with the Democratic Party saw immediately how disrespectful and harmful they were. ESPN commentator Stephen Smith had begun to wade more into politics during Biden's reelection and was saying the quiet part out loud. To his credit, he was elevating how many Democrats—more so Americans—felt about Biden being the Democratic nominee.

"I don't think it was a very wise statement on her part," Stephen Smith said on CNN shortly thereafter. "The last thing you need to do is anything that would agitate a potential voter," he concluded.

Hillary Clinton's comments underscore just how out of touch she was with the general American public and their concerns. If she had her finger on the pulse or had viewed the most recent Pew Research Center poll, she would have known that two-thirds of Americans had little or no confidence Biden was physically fit to do the job. The same poll said roughly 62 percent of Biden's own supporters would replace him and Trump on the ballot if they had the ability.

This poll was not an outlier, and voters had been very clear on how disappointed they were with Biden's decision to run again. They also had negative views on Trump's efforts to reclaim the Republican nomination. The main difference was Republican surrogates were not going on late night television, insulting their voters. They weren't telling them to "get over themselves" when their concerns about their candidate's age or fitness for office were legitimate.

It may have not been surprising that such comments would come from Hillary Clinton. Afterall, she coined the term "deplorable" during the 2016 election, castigating Trump supporters and, effectively, contributing to her historic loss. So this likely surprised few.

Hillary Clinton is a very well-accomplished individual who

has championed some incredibly noble causes during her time in public service. I have great admiration for her husband, former President Bill Clinton, and all he has given to this country. I'm also reminded of the saying my dad used to tell me, which is "Second only to what you do there, the most important part of being anywhere is knowing when to leave."

Two things can be true. One can admire a political figure for their work and accomplishments *and* acknowledge their time in the sun has passed. Those two are not mutually exclusive. The reality is the Democratic Party and the brand would be much better off if Hillary Clinton had ended her career with her presidential defeat. The lessons that should have been learned from her 2016 campaign of disparaging voters and talking down to people obviously were not. She lacked the humility that her husband possessed.

Hillary's "deplorables" comment are well etched in the annals of political history. Right beside it are the words President Biden uttered weeks before the 2024 election.

In late October 2024, during a Trump rally at Madison Square Garden, comedian Tony Hinchcliffe made insulting comments about Puerto Ricans, referring to the United States territory as "a floating island of garbage." This caused a media frenzy with every pundit pontificating on its effect on the upcoming election and how important a voting bloc Puerto Ricans are. In effect, Democrats were given yet again another opportunity to capitalize on a gaffe/error but they failed spectacularly.

Shortly following Hinchcliffe's insult, and while speaking to a group of Latino supporters, President Biden said "The only garbage I see floating out there is his supporters…"

Not good.

Biden's staff attempted to edit the transcript so the quote was not as harmful as it originally sounded but the damage had been done. This was almost as thoughtless and harmful as Hillary's "deplorable" comment back in 2016. Trump and his campaign immediately seized upon it, even staging a photo op with him by a garbage truck.

The Harris-Walz campaign was littered with slights, directly and indirectly, at Trump and his supporters. For no reason whatsoever, on October 22, 2024, Tim Walz was speaking at a rally in Wisconsin and decided to set his sights on Trump's supporter, donor, and the world's richest man: Elon Musk. During recent weeks, Musk had become more politically active and very vocal about his support for the Trump campaign. The endorsement of Musk was very impactful, and the financial support made him quite a force. Also, his backing underlined the support of that demographic with which Harris was still struggling: white men.

When addressing Musk's support of Trump, Walz told the crowd Elon was at a recent rally on stage with Trump and "jumping around, skipping like a dipshit. . ." This was completely unnecessary and an unforced error. Utterly foolish. With insulting, name-calling, he lowered himself to the level of Donald Trump.

The upside was Walz received an applause line and perhaps a few headlines. The downside was that he attacked: 1) the world's richest man, 2) a megadonor, 3) owner of X, which boasts 335 million users worldwide, 4) owner of Tesla that sells hundreds of thousands of electric cars each year in the United States, 5) owner of SpaceX, and 6) a white male (a key demographic Democrats needed).

Political attacks can come back to bite you. And this is one that did against the Harris campaign. William Shakespeare, in *Henry VIII*, wrote, "Heat not a furnace for your foe so hot that it do singe yourself." Self-inflicted wounds can be the most dangerous but also the easiest to prevent.

If the party wants to connect with voters, it must first relearn how to speak to them. Meet them wherever they are: on TV, in church, or at breweries. And for the love of God, do not insult their intelligence. Otherwise, they will be sure to show you how smart they really are. At the ballot box.

Any of these past mistakes made by the Democratic Party or its allies can be overcome. None of this is insurmountable and the party of JFK and FDR can easily rediscover and deploy a message that connects with ordinary Americans.

So long as the message is not lost by the messenger.

8

THE GERIATRIC OLIGARCHY

An aged person is like a library full of volumes of wisdom.

—UNKNOWN

Sometime in July 2024, Congresswoman Kay Granger of Texas, unbeknownst to colleagues, cast her last vote in the U.S. House of Representatives. Although her social media accounts and office would remain active for the next several months, she did not show up for work. In December 2024, five months after her last vote was cast, it was reported that she had been residing in a senior care facility since July and suffering from "dementia issues." She was still an elected representative, drawing a government salary and representing over 700,000 people from the 12th Congressional District of Texas.

I have great empathy for the family of Congresswoman Granger and understand the emotional toll such a diagnosis can take on the patient and loved ones. As a public servant, this matter does become a public one. It is not her condition, specifically, but how a sitting member of Congress can be afflicted with dementia, stop working, move into a healthcare facility without anyone noticing. What is more surprising is that this is not more surprising.

There are many conclusions one can draw from this episode, but one is evidently clear: Congress is old. In fact, it's about as old as it has ever been.

Politicians hardly ever retire. Instead, we bear witness to the physical aging process and the cognitive decline on national television and in real time. Cameras are always around to catch the slightest misstep.

Back in March 2023, Sen. Mitch McConnell, then eighty-one years old, fell at a private dinner, suffering a concussion and minor rib fracture that led to his hospitalization. Just four months after, at a press conference, he froze for approximately twenty seconds before being escorted away. The next month a similar instance occurred when he was in Covington, Kentucky, and a reporter asked a question. He appeared to freeze for thirty seconds. Every one of these instances sparked media attention as to his health and the overall age of our elected officials.

On February 10, 2025, Congressman John Larson was on the House floor delivering a speech when he abruptly paused for twenty-five seconds and became unresponsive. His staff initially blamed the incident on an adverse reaction to new medication, but it was later revealed he had suffered a complex partial seizure.

The late Sen. Dianne Feinstein had her public share of medical issues, both mental and physical. It was widely discussed how in her later years while serving in the Senate she heavily relied on aides and became confused in conversations or hearings. "She's gone," one elected official from California told me in 2022 when I was out on the West Coast. "I've seen her multiple times recently and she can't even remember who I am," he said. In July 2023, it was uncovered that her daughter had power-of-attorney over her legal and financial affairs. A sitting United States senator who made some of the most consequential decisions in our country was not even capable of making her own personal legal and financial decisions. She could vote to send our country to war, but was incapable of signing a check on her own account.

In an interview with *Politico*, Congressman Jim Himes stated, "There's no question that somewhere between six and a dozen of my colleagues are at a point where they're...I think they don't have the faculties to do their job."

Of course, as the perceptive columnist, Kathleen Parker, pointed out, the most recent and prominent exhibition of an aging office holder is former President Joe Biden. As she captured perfectly the apprehension most Americans feel about the former President, "At times I think, oh, whew, he got through that speech pretty well. I'm always pulling for him because he's our president. I want him to be strong; I wish him good health and strong knees. But at other times, his speech is so muddled, I have no idea what he's saying, and it seems he doesn't either." While always prone to gaffes, his became much more pronounced as the commander-in-chief. Throughout his term as president, he would often slip up and confuse people's names and titles. At a NATO summit, he referred to the president of Ukraine as President Putin.

During the investigation of how President Biden handled classified documents, special agent Hur released his report that highlighted Biden's cognitive decline. It was an excuse for foregoing prosecution. In the report, Biden was described as "a sympathetic, well-meaning, elderly man with a poor memory." Names and faces would often escape him. In July 2024, Congressman Seth Moulton, a Democrat from Massachusetts, revealed how President Biden did not seem to recognize him at a small gathering and it was a "crushing realization" about the president's age.

It was not just what we heard from President Biden, it was what we saw. In March 2021, he took a couple different spills while navigating the stairs up Air Force One. If it were an isolated event, it would be unfair to impugn his physical condition based only on that incident. But he fell again and by mid-2023 he was using the rear stairs of the aircraft, which are much shorter and easier than the traditional eighteen-foot-tall stairs located at the front of the aircraft. During a bike ride in June 2022, he fell over in front of reporters while trying to dismount. Optics matter. Despite these falls, gaffes, and other blatant cues of his gerontocracy, those around him refused to concede that it was perhaps time for him to pass the torch.

An owner of a pharmacy in Washington DC acknowledged filling prescriptions for members of Congress, including medications for conditions like Alzheimer's. "They're making the highest laws of the land and they might not even remember what happened yesterday," the pharmacist remarked in 2017.

We worry. We worry about them. We worry greatly about our country these moldering people lead. These examples are merely scratching the surface of the geriatric oligarchy that runs our government. And these are just the ones we know about.

Another glaring problem with aging office holders is their inability to keep up with the times. It is imperative our leaders have the physical and mental stamina to perform some of the most important work for the safekeeping of our country. Equally important is whether an aging Congress can truly grasp the quickly developing issues our country and the world are experiencing.

In 2018, Meta CEO Mark Zuckerberg testified in front of a joint U.S. Senate committee hearing concerning "Facebook, Social Media Privacy, and the Use and Abuse of Data." Much of what transpired at this hearing has been forgotten. Save for one exchange. The eighty-four-year-old Republican Senator from Utah asked Zuckerberg, "How do you sustain a business model in which users don't pay for your service?" Zuckerberg responded directly, "Senator, we run ads." The response went viral because it showcased the lack of understanding a sitting senator had on the operation of a social media app for which the committee was attempting to regulate.

Back in 2006, Congress was debating the issue of net neutrality, whether internet service providers could have the right to throttle—or speed up—service for a particular website creating an unlevel playing field on the internet. At the Senate Commerce Committee, the late Chairman Ted Stevens, who was eighty-six years old at the time, was explaining what the internet was and said, "The internet is not something that you just dump something on. It's not a big truck. It's a series of tubes."

In 2023, TikTok's CEO testified in front of the House Judiciary Committee on the issues of data practices and online security. Rep. Richard Hudson asked him, "Does TikTok access the home Wi-Fi network?" At another House hearing in 2020, Congressman Jim Sensenbrenner, then seventy-six years old, asked Meta CEO Mark Zuckerberg why Twitter had taken down posts from Donald Trump, even though Facebook does not own Twitter. These questions showed a fundamental lack of knowledge of how the platforms operate, who owns them or, worse, both.

The above examples illustrate many of our leaders do not understand some of the problems within Big Tech that need to be addressed or, sadder, how they operate. Yet, the problem doesn't stop there. If these members struggle with social media apps, how do we think they will digest a topic like Bitcoin, artificial intelligence, or other new industries?

As healthcare, education, trade, and technology have rapidly evolved, it has left many Americans in the dust. So there is a concern that aging leaders will not be able to craft and pass legislation tailored at emerging technologies and systems. However, Americans might be able to excuse having geriatric representation if their performance is satisfactory.

But has that been the case?

The short answer is no.

American politics is as toxic and divisive as it has ever been in modern history. A Pew research analysis showed Democrats and Republicans are further apart than any time in the last fifty years. Some of this can be attributed to politics "hollowing out the middle." Back in 1970, there were more than a hundred and sixty moderate Democrats and Republicans in Congress. Compare that to about a dozen or so that exist now. And it is not so easy for any ordinary American to launch a campaign and oust these uncooperative, partisan representatives.

Campaigns have become much more costly in the last several decades. The Supreme Court case *Citizens United* opened the floodgates for financial influence on today's elections. In the

1992 presidential election, both major party candidates spent a combined four-hundred million dollars. In 2024, Vice President Kamala Harris alone raised and spent over one billion dollars in just four months. Partisan gridlock has yielded more frequent and longer government shutdowns in recent years. By nearly every metric, our political system has experienced a steady decline.

And it's the people who have suffered.

The cost of our nation's healthcare has increased 300 percent in the last thirty years yet we still rank lower than most developed nations. Because of this, medical debt has become the number one reason for bankruptcy in our nation. As for our education system, costs have increased 200–300 percent in the last three decades. Americans have amassed nearly two trillion dollars of student loan debt, holding back millions of Americans from spending their money on growing their families or careers.

The American Dream for millions of Americans has been pushed further out of reach the last thirty years. Stagnant wages and increased costs have rendered the possibility of home ownership futile for so many. Women have seen their own reproductive freedoms limited since the fall of *Roe v. Wade* and the Democrats' inability or unwillingness to codify the same when they had the votes to do so.

Reasonable minds can differ as to whether racial relations have gotten better or worse in the last few decades. What is clear is that economic racial disparities have largely remained unchanged or gotten worse. Minority groups continue to experience higher poverty rates and lower wages compare to white Americans.

It's not just Americans that have suffered, but America as well. Our national debt has gone from about four trillion dollars in 1994 to over thirty-one trillion dollars in 2024. Our interest payments on that debt account for over 8 percent of our country's budget and the Congressional Budget Office estimates it could amount to 15 percent by 2040.

All of this is to simply say those who have held the reins of power the last several decades have produced results that are less than satisfactory. More bluntly, it is easy to draw the conclusion that the situation of our country and the hardships Americans face have become much worse due to the stale leadership the last several decades. Yet, many of them remain in power. Absent laws that demand their retirement, they will have little incentive to leave on their own accord.

However, they do not and death seems to be the only escape hatch for some of our country's career politicians. Their expiring in office is heartbreaking for their friends, family and colleagues. However, the impact of their deaths in office has had a profound impact that will impact generations to come.

Consider this example.

On July 4, 2025, President Trump signed into law the Big Beautiful Bill, a piece of legislation that was insistently lambasted by the Democratic Party and left-leaning media. The Congressional Budget Office, a non-partisan federal agency, estimated it would add about $3.3 trillion to our national debt, cut funds to SNAP (also known as food stamps), and take away healthcare for some ten million Americans. This mammoth piece of legislation passed the House by just one vote, 215–214. One. Single. Vote.

The day before the bill was voted on, news broke that Democratic Congressman Gerry Connelly had passed away. He was seventy-five years old and had been battling cancer. Just a couple months before, Congressman Raul Grijalva of Arizona passed away from cancer as well. Earlier that same month, Democratic Congressman Sylvester Turner also left this earth at the age of seventy. I knew Gerry well, he was an upstanding member and a noble man. I served for two years on the Natural Resources Committee with Raul, who was incredibly polite, respectful, and caring. Great men, the loss of which were deeply felt.

Apart from our emotional reactions, it must be noted that there is also a practical and consequential effect to these losses. All three of their seats remained vacant right before and months after the critical vote of the Big Beautiful Bill, robbing the Democratic Party of the ability to block this legislation. It would have taken just one.

And if there is one place where one vote is more important than Congress, it is the United States Supreme Court. Justice Ruth Bader Ginsberg was appointed by President Bill Clinton in 1993. In the early 2010s, many Democrats were urging her to retire due to her age and that the sitting Democratic President Obama could fill her seat with another juror of similar political ideology. She rebuffed such calls and continued to serve. While she was on the bench, conservatives held a 5–4 majority. With just a few months left in President Trump's term in September 2020, Justice Ginsberg passed away at the age of eighty-seven.

President Trump nominated conservative Amy Coney Barrett to succeed Justice Ginsberg, who was confirmed in October 2020, shifting the supreme court to a 6–3 conservative stronghold. In June 2022, the Supreme Court issued the *Dobbs* decision, which, by a vote of 5–4, overturned the abortion rights case of *Roe v. Wade*, sending these decisions back to the states to decide. Chief Justice Roberts voted not to overturn *Roe* while Justice Barrett did. Had Justice Ginsberg retired during President Obama's tenure, it can be assumed that her replacement would have voted alongside Chief Justice Roberts allowing the law of *Roe* to stand. With the fall of this landmark decision, at least a dozen states now have total abortion bans with few or no exceptions. The power of one vote cannot be overstated.

Death in office is not the only risk associated with getting old. Aging also comes with consistent health issues that require medical care and prevents members from attending votes. Back in the spring of 2023, Democratic Senator Diane Feinstein, who sat on the Senate Judiciary Committee was sidelined for approximately ten weeks. Her absence created a split committee, which prevented (or rather delayed) the confirmation of many of President Biden's judicial nominees. The work of the committee ground to a halt until she eventually returned to her committee seat with the assistance of a wheelchair.

Instances like the above, whether it be in Congress or our Supreme Court are destined to occur again. Due to the extreme gerrymandering of our country, which creates razor thin voting margins, there will surely be more critical pieces of legislation that will advance, which Democrats will be unable to stop due to one of their own open seats created by father time. I do not want to give the impression that this problem is exclusive to Democrats; however, it is worth noting that of the seven members of Congress who have died in office since 2023, all have been Democrats.

Defenders of the status quo on our geriatric oligarchy attempt to rationalize it by saying, "Let the voters decide." It's a very good point that needs to be addressed.

First, we must be realistic.

It's hard to take the keys away from your parents. Similar to aging parents refusing to concede that their senses are not sharp enough to operate a vehicle, politicians have the same reluctance to give up power. And while these members of the House and Senate are up for reelection every two and six years, respectively, ousting them is no easy chore. Despite Sen. McConnell's favorability rating in Kentucky hovering in the thirties, he returns to office. The influence of money, partisanship, and other national factors have made it nearly impossible to throw out longstanding incumbents.

For starters, elections have become less and less competitive. In 2018, only about one out of ten congressional races were deemed "toss-ups" those to be decided by five points or less. In 2022, it was even lower. There are many reasons for this lack of competition, including gerrymandering and the influence of money. As competition declines, the average age of members of congress goes up. Elections have not only become uncompetitive in the general election, but many have also become uncompetitive in the primary. In 2022, not one member of congress in Massachusetts faced a primary opponent.

Growing apathy in our country provides increasing security for incumbents. Numerous reports suggest voter apathy is widespread and growing. The percentage of Americans eligible to vote who did, in fact, vote was 63 percent in 1960 but has been falling since. Voter turnout hit 58 percent in 2024, which is even relatively high compared to past elections.

A galloping increase of uninterested citizens allows our faults to go undetected and uncorrected. Low attention to the weaknesses of our public servants assists those who are in power to remain in power. Apathy serves the incumbents like rain serves the flood.

AGE LIMITS

It seems more politicians would rather die in office than release their grip on power. In 2023, Sen. Feinstein of California passed away at age ninety. In 2024, Congressman Bill Pascrell from New Jersey died in office at the age of eighty-seven. This has become more of a pervasive problem and aging politicians must have another escape hatch from public service other than death. If they will not leave willingly and step aside for their own health and that of our country, the only other way is to regulate it by law.

Our Founding Fathers first established age considerations for Congress and the presidency but only addressed the floor and not the ceiling. After much debate at the Constitutional Convention, they decided members of the House of Representatives should be at least twenty-five years of age, Senators thirty years old, and thirty-five for the presidency. The level of maturity and experience required was tailored to the weight of the office.

In The Federalist Papers (No. 64), Alexander Hamilton advised that a higher age was required for senators than representatives because the former needed a certain level of wisdom and stability. This is one of the ways the founding fathers intended the senate to be the more deliberative body in Congress. The presidency, the highest elected office in the land, required the highest floor of the three. While there was debate as to the minimum age required, the record is void of any discussion on what the maximum should be. They likely assumed that voters would decide when a candidate was too old to stand for office. Our Founding Fathers could not predict how money and power in politics could create the problem we currently face and, consequently, did not foresee politicians hanging onto their elected office well into their twilight years.

Age limits are not uncommon in the United States. Airline pilots are forced to retire at age sixty-five. Air traffic controllers are forced out at age fifty-six. Federal law enforcement officers must retire at age fifty-seven. Large corporations force out CEOs and chairmen all the time under the guise of "succession planning" or "leadership transition." Age limits for public officials may be less common, but they do exist. For example, judges in South Carolina have a mandatory retirement age of seventy-two, yet none for state legislators. This leads to an obvious question: if seventy-two is too old to interpret the law, why is it not too old to make the law?

From a scientific standpoint, things begin to break down as our bodies grow old. Neurons are lost, which leads to significant changes to the brain and a decrease in function. Areas most impacted are the hippocampus (learning and memory), the frontal lobe (problem-solving, judgment control, speech) and the temporal lobe (information processing). It becomes more difficult to multi-task, to learn new abilities. While the procedural memory (like riding a bike) is less impacted, the prospective memory (remembering something for the future) takes a hit. All of this is, of course, exacerbated by age-related diseases. We should trust the science and consider these impacts and what they are having on our elected officials, especially when they play out in front of us on live television.

We must make an important point here. Age has its place in the greatness of America.

The aging are just as important to our country as our youth but just in different roles. Reportedly, after Vice President Lyndon B. Johnson had attended his first cabinet meeting he ran into his aging mentor, House Speaker Sam Rayburn. He was almost giddy with his excitement of President Kennedy's brilliant minds sitting at the center of power. Johnson gave Rayburn a litany of all the educational achievements and a display of genius on behalf of the new cabinet members. He was awed by their education, knowledge, and youth. After his glowing and excited report to Speaker Sam, the latter replied, "All that you say might be true, Lyndon, but I'd feel a whole lot better if just one of them had run for sheriff."

How many times have I seen the young, unexperienced, recent graduates of Ivy League schools hovering around the high and the mighty and I wish that just one "had run for sheriff."

Personally, I witnessed the wisdom that accompanied my former colleague, Congressman Jim Clyburn. Hearing him speak, his tone and words were most always chosen carefully and seldom used to fan the flames of partisanship. Instead, he left room for compromise with the opposing side. This is the approach that, undoubtedly, had been refined by years of experience. Yet, all things in life have their trade-offs.

In other words, what nature takes away, it replenishes. There is no substitute for experience, which brings valuable common sense and wisdom. These are qualities the elderly can contribute to our great democracy until they die. Yet, we see very little presence of gray hair and lined faces serving as advisors to our younger office holders. How many reassuring pictures have you seen of our sitting presidents in close conference with those survivor predecessors to their staggering responsibility? If I were president of the United States, I'd have every former president on speed dial.

It's a matter of record that when President Kennedy was dealing with the staggering problem of the Cuban Missile Crisis in October 1962, the young president was not only smart. He was also wise. He continually briefed and conferred with all the former presidents, even though the ancient Herbert Hoover was in his nineties.

Young parents can gain mightily by listening to aging

grandparents. So can our nation by having ample senior citizens inside their circle of power. Our younger leaders provide the energy and power to the ship of state. The elderly provide the ballast.

TERM LIMITS

More popular than age limits with the American people are term limits. In fact, recent polls have shown that anywhere between 66 percent and 80 percent of Americans support term limits for members of Congress. Many believe long-term incumbency ultimately leads to corruption, career politicians, and a dearth of new ideas.

Term limits do exist in Congress, but not on the Democratic side.

House Republicans have self-imposed term limits for their committee chairs or ranking members when they are in the minority. They have set a three-term limit, which is six years. The rule was created to generate fresh ideas and new leadership. Although the rule can be waived, it is rare.

Congressman Bennie Thompson became the ranking member of the Homeland Security committee in 2005 and held the position until 2007, when he was elected Chair and served in that role until 2011. He returned to the role of ranking member until 2019 when Democrats retook the majority, and he served as Chair until 2023 when he returned to ranking member. That's a total of twenty years a Democrat has been their party's leader on a committee compared to the six years that are typical of Republicans.

Former Governor Mark Sanford warned me of this. Prior to being sworn in, my predecessor left a note for me. In it, he warned of the dangers and pitfalls he personally witnessed of other members sacrificing everything to chase a leadership position within their party or on a committee. He told me of colleagues that had given up so much. Their child's baseball games, birthdays, anniversaries, and a litany of personal milestones, all of which were much more important in the grand scheme of things.

Upon entering Congress, I saw it firsthand. The members who would give out unlimited checks if it helped advance their pathway to a chairmanship. The endless favors extended to colleagues to earn goodwill and, ultimately, their vote when leadership is elected. It takes hard work to aspire to these positions, but sometimes folks get lost in the journey. They forget the reason that brought them into public service in the first place. They become too well accustomed to the pleasures and comforts of living in the spotlight.

Some within the Democratic Party simply refuse to let go of the reins of leadership for fear of losing the grand office, the black SUV that swoops them up, or the endless attention they receive from the media. Democrat Jim Clyburn reiterated this when back in May 2025 in a piece for *The Wall Street Journal.* The eighty-three-year-old was asked if retirement was something he would entertain in the near. He responded, "What do you want? Me to give up my life?" Most of us would likely feel the same if in their position. It does not make it right and it does not mean it should be ignored or swept under the rug.

Despite term limits being extremely popular among Americans, it is very unlikely they ever become law. First, it would take members of Congress voting against their own interest, which they are typically not inclined to do. It would require two-thirds vote in both the House and the Senate and subsequently need to be ratified by three-quarters of the state legislatures. It is an incredibly high bar. The last time it occurred was the 27th Amendment, which states any increase in pay for Congress will not take place until the next representatives are elected. Even that law took two hundred years to pass as James Madison originally proposed it in 1789 in the original Bill of Rights.

America stands apart on the world stage with its aging leaders. The Democratic Party has done little to help the situation, only exacerbated it. It would be easier to forgive if the financial health of our country and its citizens had been steadily increasing decade after decade but that has not been the case. How is it such an incredible country has allowed leaders to remain in power even when the results would swiftly warrant their dismissal?

America has made incredible strides in her young life. Tom Brokaw coined the term "Greatest Generation" to describe those who had grown up in the Great Depression and then went on to fight in World War II. After, our country enjoyed tremendous growth and prosperity and, eventually, expansion of civil rights to African Americans who had been historically oppressed. The progress made by one generation can be very different from the progress made by the following. I'm reminded of the quote by G. Michael Hopf, which reads:

Hard times create strong men.
Strong men create good times.
Good times create weak men.
Weak men create hard times.

If it is going to thrive, the Democratic Party needs new leadership and new ideas. It must have a firm understanding on the hardships millions of Americans have been placed under the last number of years and put forward commonsense solutions to the same. It must acknowledge that we also face new problems through the internet, AI, and evolving technology and we must control it before it controls us. The leaders of yesterday will not be able to provide the answers of tomorrow.

New messengers will be necessary for the Democratic Party to thrive. Ones who can focus on the most pressing, kitchen-table issues and dispel the culture wars that have stolen the Party's focus while costing it elections in the process.

9

THE COST OF CULTURE WARS

The promise of America is not equality of outcomes, but we must have equality of opportunity.

—CONDOLEEZZA RICE

In the award-winning movie of 1960 *Inherit the Wind* there is a powerful scene at the end. Henry Drummond, played by Spencer Tracy, is an old lawyer who is summing up the life of his old friend Matthew Brady, who has just died. They were both lawyers and had been close friends. But they had become estranged in their last years over their sharp disagreement over the teaching of evolution in the public schools. Brady had grown fanatically narrow minded and rigid in his final days.

But Drummond was neither ungrateful nor vengeful about his departed friend. "A giant once lived in that body," he said of Brady. "But he got lost looking for God too high up and too far away."

There was a giant who lived in the Democratic Party at one time. But the Party has lost its way, looking for needs too high up and too far away. Chasing causes and issues that affect a very small percentage of Americans. It has spent too much time in the world of ivory tower liberals who are worried about the weeds in the yard while there is no bread in the cupboard. They never shop at Walmart, drink coffee at Roy's Cafe, attend church with farmers and factory workers, and never are late on their mortgage payments because the breadwinner's job went to Mexico.

We took care of these people once, but we started looking for God too high up and too far away. The Party's gaze has drifted beyond the basic needs like healthcare, housing, and education and has settled on a culture war that includes gender identity, racial quotas, DEI, and bathrooms. As a result, it has cost them swaths of voters who may never come back.

One of the biggest self-inflicted injuries of the Democratic Party has resulted from prioritizing gender identity above nearly everything else.

The LGBT community has made remarkable strides for equality in such a short period of time. Undoubtedly, millions of Americans have faced discrimination based solely on who they love. Just a decade ago, some states refused to recognize same-sex marriage, and now it is a protected right in all fifty. In 2020, the Supreme Court ruled that Title VII of the Civil Rights Act of 1964 protects LGBTQ+ employees from workplace discrimination, making it illegal to fire someone based on sexual orientation or gender identity. Many states have passed legislation expanding protections for the LGBTQ+ community as it relates to housing and healthcare. Our courts have increasingly recognized the rights of same sex couples as it pertains to adoptions and parental rights. Much ground has been gained and still more to cover.

The transgender community continues to garner the most attention in their path to progress and equality. In our effort to cure discrimination, we sometimes reach too far. Many people in this country are battered by discrimination and should be defended by the shield of the law.

It is worth distinguishing between protection and privilege. There is a difference, after all, in leveling the playing field and tilting it. To highlight an example, here is the rule that governs how the officers of the South Carolina Democratic Party are to be elected:

The First Vice Chair shall be of a gender different from the Chair, the Second Vice Chair shall be of a race different from the Chair, and the Third Vice Chair shall be at least 18 years old and shall not have reached thirty-six years of age.

Based on the above, if you identify as transgender, you can run for First Vice Chair no matter if the Chair is male, female, or transgender. If the Chair is a female, a female is prohibited from running for First Vice Chair. Or vice versa. As of 2024, there is no male representation among its officers. Gender or gender identity is used in the selection of the Executive Committee as well, according to Section IV.2A, which states:

The State Executive Committee shall be composed of two members, one man and one woman, or someone of a different gender identity, from each county, to be elected every two years by the County Conventions. Each county may elect two Alternate members, one man and one woman, or someone of a different gender identity who shall represent the county in the absence of the Executive Committee Members.

So goes for the Executive Council with Section IV.3:

The Council shall be composed of two members, one man and one woman, or someone of a different gender identity from each Congressional District and the Chair of the State Party who shall be Chair of the Council.

Even during a vacancy, gender or gender identity is the controlling factor in the selection, according to Section V6:

In the event that the office of the State Executive Committee Person shall become vacant, the Alternate Executive Committee person of the same gender as the vacating Executive Committeeperson shall become the replacement Executive Committeeperson to the State Executive Committee.

In prescribing how county conventions elect their delegates, Section V1.1(F) states:

Half the delegates must be female and half male; the same is required of the alternates when possible. Persons of other gender identities chosen as delegates or alternates do not affect these ratios.

It is lost upon me how the rules provide strict quotas for men and women but treats "persons of other gender identities" in a way that "do not affect these ratios." Men and women have strict numbers on what offices they can hold and how many, but the same does not apply to those of different gender identities. Affording this group more rights than males or females is in no way fair and has the potential of creating resentment. The Party's eagerness to rectify past discriminations against these groups has led them to step right onto the toes of everyone else and their individual liberties. Personal rights, after all, end when they begin to infringe upon the rights of others.

Allowing men to play in women's sports is an example.

MEN IN WOMEN'S SPORTS

Ms. Riley Gaines was a collegiate swimmer from the University of Kentucky who, when competing in the NCAA Women's Swimming Championship in March 2022, tied for 5th Place with Lia Thomas. Thomas, a transgender athlete, was a member of the University of Pennsylvania's men's swim team and had been ranked sixth fastest in the nation in the one-thousand-yard freestyle. After two years competing under the men's banner, Thomas began transitioning to a female and joined the women's team for the 2021–2022 swim season, when Thomas bested Gaines.

The event sparked a debate on women's sports and whether men who have or are transitioning to be a woman should be allowed to compete in women's sports. Gaines claimed the NCAA gave the trophy to Lia to make a statement on inclusivity. Since then, Ms. Gaines has been a fierce advocate on this matter while the issue has become a political liability for Democrats up and down the ballot.

There have been more and more instances of biological men playing in women's sports and not only winning, but sometimes injuring women in the process. Payton McNabb, a female high school volleyball player was injured when an alleged biological male spiked a ball, striking her face and injuring her neck and back, sidelining her for the remainder of the season. Stories like these strike a nerve in nearly every American with a family, particularly those with daughters who wish to play sports without the fear of serious injury.

Republicans found this not only makes good policy, but good politics and the Democrats were caught flat footed against these political attacks. During the 2024 presidential election cycle Trump and Republicans spent two-hundred and fifteen million dollars on this issue while claiming in a hyper-effective TV ad that "Kamala is for they/them. Trump is for you." Many believe this specific ad injured the Harris campaign in a way they were never able to fully recover. Democrats down ballot felt the pain, too, as they were painted with a broad brush. Out of fear for crossing the small faction on the far left that was pushing for these policies, many were unable or unwilling to vocalize their opposition. To do so would be viewed as treason by the far left.

Democratic Congressman Seth Moulton found this out when he stated publicly biological men should not be playing in women's sports. He said, "I have two little girls, I don't want them getting run over on a playing field by a male or formerly male athlete, but as a Democrat I'm supposed to be afraid to say that." How were these comments received by Moulton's party? His campaign manager allegedly resigned as a result and a local university supposedly cancelled their externship program with his office. The chairman of his state's Democratic Party said, "These comments do not represent the broad view of our Party."

Is that last statement true? Is it the "broad view" or simply the loudest? Within the Democratic Party, views on gender identity differ along racial lines. One survey shows that 66 percent of Black Democrats believe that a person's sex is determined at birth while 72 percent of white Democrats believe that someone can be the opposite gender from which they were born. In my home state of South Carolina, Black Democrats make up 60 percent of the state's primary electorate so the importance of this issue should not be discounted.

Look at the Democratic Party as a whole and not just white or Black. A *New York Times* poll indicated that two-thirds of Democrats believe transgender female (i.e., born male) athletes should not be able to compete with biological female athletes. This data shows rank and file Democrats are in line with America concerning biological men playing in women's sports. The disconnect between the Democrats and the Democratic Party can be explained in one of two ways. Either its Representatives are not representative or the advocates for biological men playing in women's sports, although outnumbered, are much, much louder.

Zooming out further to the general electorate, the percentage of voters who believe biological men should not compete against women ticks up to 80 percent! Those are difficult numbers to overcome if you are a Democrat, even if you don't support that unpopular position. Like it or not, the Democratic Party has been defined by the least popular positions taken by the more extreme members of the party.

And for what or for whom?

Those Americans who identify as transgender are less than 1 percent. Many surveys approximate it to be between 0.5 percent–0.6 percent. What percentage of this number desires to play competitive sports? Or what percent believes it is fair for biological men to play in women's sports? It is likely the percentage of transgender athletes seeking to compete in women's sports is extremely low. Yet, in an effort to court this small faction, the Democratic establishment has broken with the majority of its base, abandoning a large swath of voters while looking for God too high up and too far away.

But what has caused this shift among Democrats? What encourages them to keep shoving solutions into corners where virtually no problems live? There exists an unspoken rivalry among liberals as to who can appear more inclusive or "woke."

During the 2024 presidential race, an old clip of Harris emerged where she discusses staying "woke." In it, she says, "You know, we have to stay 'woke.' Like, everybody needs to be 'woke.' And you can talk about if you're the 'wokest' or 'woker' but just be more 'woke' than less 'woke.'" The old clip garnered broad attention because "woke" had become a trigger word often associated with super progressive policies like DEI (Diversity, Equity, Inclusion), men in women's sports and bathrooms, etc.

But the part that stands out to me is how she specifically hinted that there is a competition among liberals as to who can "out-liberal" the other. "And you can talk about if you're the 'wokest' or 'woker'. . ." she says. It implies the party is pushing further left and that members take pride in announcing they are the "most woke" of their colleagues. Are you "woke enough" if you don't have a sticker on your car or your pronouns listed in your email signature line? Or a mention in your social media profile? It answers the question of how Democrats found themselves on the wrong side of these divisive issues. They raced there! And once Democrats got there, they were trapped and have turned the ball over to Republicans.

While playing high school basketball, we would travel to many old gymnasiums around western Kentucky. Servicing small high schools of anywhere between two hundred and a thousand students, these timeworn gyms possessed the same hardwood floors and fixtures for decades. As we would begin warming up, our coach would take a basketball, pace back and forth, and meticulously bounce it on every square foot of the floor. As the ball struck the hardwood, his ear would follow, listening and feeling as the ball returned to him. As we did lay-up lines and three-man weave, he would continue bouncing the ball on the court like a mental patient.

In the huddle, Coach would mark with an "X" on his markerboard where our defense would aim to trap the opposing team in a full or half-court press. The rationale was to steer the other team to these dead spots on the gym floor—parts where the wood beneath was worn or rotten—and then trap. Oftentimes it worked as the ball would take a bad bounce near that dead spot, the other team would lose the dribble and turn the ball over.

Steer the other team to the weak spots and then trap.

It's a similar strategy rolled out by the Republican Party, as they have welcomed Democrats into a culture war and the Democratic Party has willingly walked into it. In January 2025, House Republicans put up a bill titled "Protection of Women and Girls in Sports Act" which garnered two Democratic votes. The Republican Party has been successful at identifying issues that not only divide America, but divide the Democratic Party. And then they apply pressure and amplify in the media. The press, particularly the conservative media, has been effective at extracting the most liberal legislation from a blue corner of our country and bringing it up to DC to hang around the necks of every Democrat.

In California, the School Success and Opportunity Act, which passed in 2013, enshrined the rights of pupils to join sports teams based upon their gender identity, not what was on their birth certificate. In nearly half of the other states, legislatures have passed laws effectively banning participation in sports opposite from a student's birth gender. At federal, state, and even down to the local level at school board hearings, Republicans have welcomed this debate. They have guided Democrats to where they wanted them to go and trapped them, knowing the public sentiment weighs heavily in their favor. Most Democrats know they are on shaky ground but fear a loud minority within their party turning on them and being labeled some form of *ism* or *ist*.

It would be unfair to place all the fault of identity politics squarely at the feet of the Democratic Party. The left-leaning media shares just as much blame, if not more. For reasons solely aligned with profit, they have surrendered headlines to these narratives and will often find a racial or gender manner to shape a story simply because it sells. There exists a symbiotic relationship between the Democratic Party and the left-leaning media, like slack being let out on a leash and a dog running further. Both entities working in parallel, neither realizing how far away they are running and their ideological views straying from the common American.

THE ISSUE OF RACE

In the 2020 cycle, Congressman Joe Kennedy made the ambitious decision to run in the primary against sitting Massachusetts Democratic Senator Ed Markey. Joe is sharp, articulate, and was a very likable member of Congress with an exemplary record of results. The contrast between his young face and his Democratic opponent's would have been impactful had COVID not suppressed his ability to connect in-person with voters.

As customary with challengers, Joe sat down with various editorial boards to answer the typical questions: *Why are you running? What are you going to do for our constituents? Why do you think you're better than the alternative?* The goal in these meetings is to get to know each other but, as a candidate, ultimately gain the publication's endorsement.

Joe sat down with representatives from *The Boston Globe* and one writer bluntly asked, "What are you going to do if you are elected and later a Black female challenges you in the next race?"

Joe was a bit stunned and followed up, "What do you mean?"

"Well, would you still run against her?" the editor asked.

"Yeah," Joe answered laughing it off, but underneath realizing the depths of identity politics the party had sunk.

Even Joe, a liberal politician from Massachusetts was a bit taken back by the proposition. The insinuation that he, as a white male, was expected to withdraw from a race or give up his seat if a Black female—any Black female—threw her hat into the ring. The interaction exemplifies how far identity politics has taken the Democratic Party away from the rest of America. Asking a qualified candidate to bow out and surrender to anyone because of skin color or gender does nothing to bridge the racial or gender divide, it only broadens it.

The far left of the Democratic Party is pulling us farther and farther away from reaching the dream of Martin Luther King, Jr., "I have a dream that my four little children will one day live in a nation where they will not be judged by the color of their skin but by the content of their character."

During my gubernatorial run in 2022, my main primary opponent was a Black female state senator from Columbia, over a hundred miles away from where I lived. I sought out endorsements from county Party chairs and elected officials, but even those in my back yard were reluctant. Looking back, I can count those endorsements on one hand. The vast majority told me that they could not publicly endorse a white male over a Black female. This spoke volumes of the Party and how frozen in fear many were of just the optics of competing against a person of color.

This baseless fear within the Party and its members was once again amplified by the narrative pushed by the media. On the day of the Democratic primary in 2022, *The Washington Post* ran a story with the headline "In South Carolina, race and gender animate Democratic gubernatorial primary." It was a lazy and intellectually dishonest headline and the left-leaning media shares some of the blame for elevating racial politics within the Democratic Party. Oftentimes, they reach for a racial element because it garners more attention and receives more clicks. Ultimately, I bested the state senator by twenty-five points, avoiding a runoff in a five-way primary.

The Democrats' ticket for the 2024 election was shaped by racial politics. Upon Biden withdrawing from the race, there was a sliver of time when some thought an open primary would serve the Party well in determining who would take on Trump. It was widely accepted within Democratic circles that any challenge to a Black woman for the nomination would be viewed as sexist and/or racist. The party had a deep bench of talented and well-spoken leaders who could have injected much needed enthusiasm into the race. However, the party allowed racial politics to dictate its presidential nominee. Left-leaning media supported the idea that race and gender should lead the discussion. Upon Biden exiting the race, CNN published a story with the headline "Harris will seek the Democratic nomination and could be the first Black woman and Asian American to lead a major party ticket."

I had numerous discussions, all of which had a consistent theme, which was this: *Anyone openly challenging Harris's ascension to the throne would be painted as racist or sexist and likely both. A large voting bloc of the party was Black and they would be insulted if she was passed over and someone of a different color was chosen. Further, any candidate who might challenge her or even suggest an open primary would ruin his/her future within the Party and if they had presidential aspirations, they would be wise to sit on them until 2028.*

Upon extinguishing any hope of a Democratic process for selecting the Democratic presidential nominee, attention was then placed on who the nominee should be for vice president. Racial and gender politics drove this decision as well. As opposed to nominating the best possible candidate, the liberal media and national Democrats essentially restricted the field of applicants to white males. It was openly discussed on news segments that Harris needed a white male to "balance the ticket." Talking heads did not even attempt to disguise the blatant bias behind the selection of a person that might be one heartbeat away from leading the strongest nation on earth. Policy, enthusiasm, experience nor any other factor was prioritized over race and gender. For the Party and the networks that strive for diversity, there could be none found in the field of applicants for second in command.

One of the driving forces behind racial politics within the Democratic Party is diversity, which is well-intended. Diversity in race, gender, and thought are all beneficial. In law school, a Black student who lived in a predominately Black neighborhood was sharing with the Criminal Procedures class some nuggets about her neighborhood. When any friends were coming over, she told them first to expect to be pulled over by the cops and possibly searched when entering her neighborhood. As a white male, the notion of an "unreasonable search and seizure" is not something to which I'd been personally exposed. And if you're not exposed to it, it is easy to assume that for anyone who gets pulled over or searched, there was good reason.

Growing up in Kentucky with an 8 percent Black population, there are many parts of the culture to which I was never exposed. Trailers—single and doublewide—white rednecks, good ol' boys: I've seen my fair share of these. But I've never had to have "the talk" with my son when he gets his driver's license, and I've never been eyed or followed around in a convenience store. Nor have I been subjected to "unreasonable searches and seizures." Even though I'll never know what these things truly feel like, I do know they exist and can empathize.

The issue arises when diversity supplants all else and overtakes common sense. The Democratic Party is hemorrhaging supporters who feel the party places diversity over merit. Many feel if a hire is announced and it leads with the person's color, gender, or sexual orientation, then that is the reason they were hired as opposed to their qualifications.

Before South Carolina's Democratic presidential primary in 2020, Biden made the promise to nominate a Black woman to the nation's highest court. It was well-received among his base, as the Court had never held a jurist of that gender and color. In doing so, Biden narrowed his choices considerably. At the time, there were only five Black women serving on the U.S. Appeals Court, the pool from which most supreme court justices are drafted. All of them were over the age of sixty-eight, which can be a deterrent if you wish that Justice to have a long tenure on the highest court. Restricting his pool of applicants was not the issue; it was how the message was received by others.

By announcing such a litmus test for one of the country's most important offices, Biden eliminated 90 percent of duly qualified candidates. In other words, disregarding the dream of Martin Luther King, Jr., he also denied an overwhelming number of eligible and qualified Americans the right to be considered for membership on the U.S. Supreme Court.

When I speak with neighbors and friends who reliably vote Democratic, specifically white men and women, they feel as if race is being placed ahead of merit, all to correct the wrongs with which they, nor their parents, had anything to do with.

Justice Ketanji Brown Jackson completed her undergraduate and law studies at Harvard, where she also served on the *Harvard Law Review*, a prestigious honor typically reserved for those with the highest academic marks. She later served as a federal public defender, which can be very challenging but delivers a great education on the justice system from within the courtroom. She served as the vice chair of the United States Sentencing Commission and then as a district judge in Washington DC. Put simply, Justice Jackson has a solid résumé and experience on which to stand. Biden could have easily highlighted any of her past achievements or records of success, tamping down any rhetoric that she was nominated solely because of her skin color or gender.

Back when he was selecting his running mate, he started the process by eliminating 50 percent of the applicants. During the presidential primary in 2020, Biden vowed to have a woman as his vice president. Senator Sanders, who was still competing for the nomination at the time, would not even make that commitment. When asked, he simply responded, "In all likelihood, I will."

Many of President Biden's announcements of hires focuses on skin color, gender, or gender identity and, as a result, suppressed what qualifications and experience they may have had. He nominated the most diverse set of judges than any other president in history. Sixty percent of his judges confirmed were non-white in a country that is 25 percent non-white.

I believe government should look like the people it serves as much as possible—but not at the expense of merit. I have reiterated the same on the campaign trail and have not restricted this concept to just race or gender, but have extended it to political views as well. In my 2022 gubernatorial bid, I also pledged to have qualified Republicans serve in my administration. Diversity at all levels has benefits. The Democratic Party would be able to harness these benefits without incurring the backlash if it simply did not lead with it and place so much public emphasis on it.

While important, diversity should not be our guiding star. For then the chances of democracy surviving are diminished. Sounds harsh, but let me explain. Freedom and democracy will exist only when there is an equal playing field. Once it is tilted, we lose our way. The American dream must be open to every citizen, guided by the measure of one's character and talents, never by skin color, gender, or religion. Diversity should be America's barometer. It should tell us how we are doing in opening America to equal opportunity to all regardless of race, gender, religion, or ethnic group.

But racial politics can be complicated. And our country has a troubled past when it comes to race relations. From our founding days that were immersed in slavery to modern-day discrimination, racial tension has plagued our nation since its birth. Certain communities have been irreparably damaged through practices like redlining. Banks and lending institutions have used this practice to limit resources in predominately Black neighborhoods. The damage that has been done has lasted generations and continues to this day. There are certain wounds like these that we, as a country, are obligated to help heal.

The question becomes *how*.

Democrats, and all Americans, should consider how best to right the wrongs of generations past. Is it through patchwork practices like affirmative action or DEI or is it through long-term investments in communities and areas that have long been neglected? The first thought would be to go inside these communities and ask them. One may find they need a grocery store, a community bank that can cater to small businesses, quality schools, well-trained police forces, high wage jobs, better modes of transportation, or any other quality of life those outside their neighborhoods take for granted. There are no shortcuts to anything in life and instilling equity is a long-term commitment.

The problem with such programs as affirmative action and quotas is that we are tilting the playing field in favor of one race over another race (or races)—one injustice replacing another. Martin Luther King, Jr., wisely proclaimed, "an injustice anywhere is a threat to justice everywhere." Ironically, it was Asian-Americans whose Supreme Court Case effectively ended affirmative action. Asian Americans had higher test scores and GPAs but were admitted at a lower rate than their peers, including whites and Blacks. All on the basis of diversity. The Court concluded it was unconstitutional, effectively ending affirmative action in the admissions of higher education.

These policies have bred resentment among parents who either felt or knew their child's seat in a school was given to another student, not based upon merit, but skin color. These experiences poke at the racial scab in our country until it bleeds.

And the very last thing we need right now is more resentment between races.

Be honest. Are you happy with race relations right now?

I'm not. I want to see more Blacks in board rooms, in banking, in the box seats at professional baseball games, playing professional tennis and golf, more doctors and lawyers.

As mentioned above, the racial injustices in our country go back a ways, forcing Blacks into less-desired neighborhoods and draining them of resources that are critical to surviving and thriving. Affirmative action, however well-intended, is a patchwork solution that avoids the root of the problem. It fails to confront the inequities Americans created and, as a result, becomes a superficial fix that ultimately widens the racial divide instead of bridging it.

The stale old policies of the Democratic Party concerning race have failed. Democrats cannot be so proud to say that every single cause they have championed has been a resounding success. That's not how businesses work, or marriages, or anything. When solutions are introduced and they fail to address a problem—particularly after decades, we have an obligation to step back and re-examine and find a way to improve upon it. We owe it to our Black brothers and sisters to do better. To do better, we have to look for better ways.

The answers to many of our problems are right there in front of us. There is no need to go looking for them too high up or too far away. No need to "out-woke" your neighbor. It's a good way to get lost. If the Democratic Party is to find itself again, it must keep its feet planted on the ground and rediscover the simple solutions that can help cure our society's more complex problems. Oftentimes, this requires one ingredient that seems to be rare in politics: courage.

10

THE PRICE OF TRUTH

It takes a great deal of bravery to stand up to our enemies, but just as much to stand up to our friends.

—J.K. ROWLING

"I don't understand why politicians just won't do the right thing. Like, why are they so scared?" I was having dinner at a political event in a swanky Manhattan penthouse when a guest announced his query. He was referring to a recent legislative vote. It could have been any of them. And he was highlighting the absence of members who would opt to break with their own political party and stand up for what's right. It is a question I had heard before in many forms and I never thought to give it a comprehensive answer, partly because it was always a question sandwiched between other questions. Until now.

Politicians raising their voice against their own party to express dissent is not commonplace. There are exceptions. Most recall when Sen. John McCain gave the famous "thumbs down" to Republicans' effort to repeal the Affordable Care Act in 2017. It infuriated those within his own party, including President Trump. But he saved healthcare for millions of Americans. Sen. Mitt Romney has shown an abundance of courage, specifically when he voted to impeach President Trump for withholding aid to Ukraine in exchange for political dirt on the Bidens. Former congresspersons Liz Cheney and Adam Kinzinger displayed much fortitude when calling out President Trump's actions (and inactions), which fanned the flames of January 6. But what about the Democrats?

During the first term of Trump's presidency, Democrats would often criticize their Republican colleagues for refusing to stand up to Trump when he made an off-color remark or proposed policies that ran counter to American values. But how common was it that Democrats themselves broke rank and stood up to their own leadership? Democrats lay claim to being the big tent party and welcoming diversity. However, my own personal experiences suggest it is not big enough and does not include diversity of thought or ideas. With the help of the liberal media, the Democratic Party is just as bad—possibly worse—than Republicans at snuffing out dissent amongst their own and ensuring everyone is in line. I say this with some personal experience.

My first step into politics was done by openly pushing back against the national Democratic Party. It was June 2017 when I announced my longshot bid to unseat Republican Congressman

Mark Sanford in South Carolina's 1st Congressional District. Jon Ossoff and Archie Parnell had just lost special elections in districts in Georgia and South Carolina, respectively. On the morning of June 17, 2017, I tweeted my announcement video and immediately followed it with a tweet saying I would not, if elected, support Nancy Pelosi as Speaker.

The media was immediately drawn to that tweet and began reposting on all major political channels. The national attention from that tweet would extend into the next day, when *The Today Show* aired an image of the tweet along with some brief coverage. For a district in the deep south that was never considered to be competitive for a Democrat, it was garnering much attention, at least for the time being. But for every headline, there were fifty comments, posts, or emails slamming my decision to not support the Democrats' leader. Although I had made it clear then and still do that this was always about bringing in new leadership, it did not seem to matter for those whose loyalties lie with Nancy Pelosi. For the following months on the campaign trail or in meetings with donors, I was reminded of how disappointed many were in this stance, oftentimes telling me they could not support my candidacy because of it.

Worth noting is how unpopular Nancy Pelosi was and is in red districts. For years she has been used as the boogeyman (or boogeywoman) by Republicans. Those in the 1st District of South Carolina were aware of this. When Mark Sanford ran against Elizabeth Colbert-Busch in a special election in 2013 for the seat, he had called a press event at the Medical University of South Carolina in downtown Charleston. When the media showed up to cover it, they were surprised to see Sanford standing behind a podium and, right beside him, a life-sized cutout of Nancy Pelosi. He began his press conference by saying, "And since [My opponent] won't debate, I'm left to debate Nancy. Nancy, where do you stand on the NLRB?" He went on to quiz the nonresponsive cardboard cutout on the stimulus and how it would affect the area. While many shook their heads at this stunt, it proved effective, and Sanford ultimately reclaimed his seat.

While I may have been the first to make this public statement of non-support for Pelosi, I was certainly not alone. Connor Lamb who ran for and won a special election in Pennsylvania in early 2018 made a similar pledge soon after I did. Other members of the 2018 class who were sworn in January 2019 made the same commitment. Following through on the promise was another matter.

The first week member-elects are in DC are for orientation and while they are finding their way around the Capitol, Nancy Pelosi was finding her way to Speaker. One by one, she would invite new members into her office to ask for their support. My number had been called just a couple days into my orientation, and I sat next to her in her office with three televisions on blasting different news channels.

"I recognize you're in the business of counting votes, and I just want you to know where I stand on the Speaker's race and that you can put me in the 'no' column," I told her.

She was incredibly respectful and asked me to keep an open mind on how I voted. Because of how Speaker votes were tallied, there was a distinct difference in voting "present" and voting for someone else. She only needed a majority of those who voted for a particular Speaker so by voting present, it would make her pathway to the gavel a bit easier.

Upon leaving her office, the pressure continued day by day until that first vote was called. Media was constantly doing a roll call on who the Democratic "no" votes were for Pelosi and trying to uncover who would emerge from the left to challenge Pelosi. No one ever emerged.

To her credit and to my knowledge, Pelosi never retaliated against me. I was never treated any different, and I suppose being new to Congress and being upfront and honest with her from the beginning helped the situation. Or it could have been that she received the gavel and simply didn't care about much else. But if I thought this would not be used against me by my own Party in some sort of way, I was extremely naïve. That brings me to the first reason why many are afraid to break ranks with leadership and stand on their own. It's all about the money.

The House Majority Pac ("HMP") is the Congressional Democrats' spending arm that helps elect democrats. Protecting incumbents, particularly the vulnerable ones, is, or should be, a top priority. While Nancy Pelosi doesn't have an official role with this PAC, it maintains close ties to her leadership circle. For instance, Mike Smith, who previously served as a senior advisor to Pelosi, was appointed as the PAC's president in January 2023. The donors to this PAC are, largely, Democratic donors familiar with the former Speaker.

As a candidate, one is not allowed to coordinate with these types of Political Action Committees ("PACs"), as they are what's considered to be the "soft side" of campaigns and the campaign itself is considered the "hard side." The rules of the Federal Election Commission prohibit it. As a result, a candidate never knows what a group like that will spend or how it will be spent. If you are a challenger in a race, you can only *hope* a group like this will help you by spending money for TV spots. If you're an incumbent, it is more likely you *expect* them to.

HMP raised and spent over a hundred and sixty million dollars in the 2020 election on behalf of Democratic Congressional candidates, with most of it used to protect incumbents. The amount a candidate spends varies wildly based upon its competitiveness and the cost of their media market. Keep in mind, due to gerrymandering, only about 5 percent of races are considered competitive in the general election. Hence, those are typically the ones targeted by HMP and other groups.

So as the election neared, many vulnerable Democrats seeking reelection in 2020 expected HMP to spend serious money on their behalf. One could expect hundreds of thousands to millions depending on the nature of one's race. Months before the 2020 election, most members were dialing in their media plan, deciding on how much to spend on paid communications and how. Word must have gotten out that many of the Democrats representing Republican districts were planning on placing Nancy Pelosi in our communications, and not in a good way. Our goal, for those of us who kept our promise to not vote for her as Speaker, was simply to remind voters of the same. Someone, somewhere did not agree.

I was alerted to the news one afternoon while walking to the House floor for votes. "Listen, this is what we're being told," my chief of staff started. "Anyone who puts her name in any of her ads should expect any funding by HMP to be completely pulled." I was amazed.

"No funding at all? Are you kidding me?" I asked. But I knew the answer. At the time, and to this day, I could not be sure if this directive or threat was coming from those close to the Speaker wanting to save her the personal embarrassment, or if it was coming from her directly. It infuriated me how this group would threaten to kneecap the most vulnerable members and threaten to withhold millions of dollars all for the purpose of saving the Speaker some embarrassment. I believed these decisions were being made by those who did not understand what it took to swing a district from red to blue and, hence, could not comprehend how bad the Democratic brand was in our races.

This decision still baffles me to this day. Stupidity is a strong word. I use it sparingly and will not use it here. But it comes to mind. Nancy Pelosi has no national aspirations. Any derision of her, no matter how harsh, in a bright red congressional district in South Carolina will not harm her politically or the Democratic Party in the least. But losing that seat to a Republican can jeopardize her position of Speaker of the House. As it turned out, my seat was lost, and the Democratic Party and Pelosi came precariously close to losing the House. I'd think the wiser response to a valued fellow Democrat would be, "Do what you have to, Joe. We need you back up here."

My team had internal discussions as to how to navigate this conundrum. As a candidate, I had the autonomy to put out whatever message I wanted with my own campaign. I believed that reminding voters I had kept my promise and stood up to Democratic leadership would bolster my campaign, particularly among swing and right-leaning voters. That would have to be weighed against possibly losing out on millions of dollars in ads purchased by HMP. It was tough to raise that level of money and thoughtful consideration needed to be given to the tradeoff before making any decision.

It was only three weeks before voters would decide whether to send me back to Congress when I reached the conclusion that it was worth reminding my constituents of my vote against Nancy Pelosi for Speaker. Before pulling the trigger, I thought it was best I let her know in person so she did not hear it from others. Also, these rumors could have had no merit to them, and her reaction to my news may suggest the same. I wanted to see for myself. Once my staff was able to arrange a short meeting, I trucked down to her office. I sat down in a chair just outside her office and she came out and took the seat beside me.

"Look, Madam Speaker," I began. "I'm sure you can appreciate my district and how tough it is. As we are looking to decide what final ads to put on TV these last few weeks, I think it is important that I remind voters how I stayed true to my word," I continued. "So I plan on reminding them of my vote for new leadership when it came to the Speaker's race." I could sense a slight irritation, so I attempted to gently massage the situation.

"What I would put on TV would not be anything personal or disparaging," I continued. "What I intend to say is that I simply kept my word. First, I wanted to tell you first so that you heard it from me. Second, I want you to assure me that after I do this there will not be any type of repercussions, and this is not something you or anyone else will hold against me." That was all I wanted to say. *I'm doing it and I don't want to get any blowback.*

"Well, I know you have all of these great accomplishments as a freshman and I think voters would want to hear about those," she countered. "Why play into their games when you have your own wins to run on? Don't allow them to dictate your moves," she continued. She made a fair point. And analyzing in a silo, it made sense. But it was hard to respond without bluntly telling her how extremely unpopular Democrats were, including her, in a state like South Carolina.

"This was a big campaign promise and so it comes back to trust with my voters and I still think it's best to make sure they know," I continued. At this time, she stood up, indicating the conversation had come to an end. "Well, you're gonna do whatever it is you're gonna do," she stated as she motioned with her hand in a circular motion with fingers spread apart, the same motion I had seen her and many other Italians make when trying to punctuate their sentences.

The meeting was over, and I walked away knowing I had said my piece—knowing I wasn't going to surprise anyone—yet still unsure where, exactly, the directive to omit Pelosi's name from our television ads had come from. For the next couple weeks, we continued to poll within our district and watch my lead over my opponent extend into double digits. Assessing my growing lead in the polls as the election neared, I made the decision not to put that message on television because it didn't seem necessary. What I did not know was how far off my polling and every other Democrats would be that election cycle.

The threat of withholding campaign funds happens every day. It can be hard dollars or it can be soft. Advocacy groups and PACs want to spend money electing or re-electing members who are sympathetic to their issues. So they will grade members on how they vote and allocate their resources accordingly. Cast the right votes and a group may put out a full-page ad in your local paper thanking you. Or they will send out thousands of mailers to your voters or put up a TV ad praising your hard work, all of which could help bolster a candidate's chance at winning the next election. There are countless ways that money will melt away someone's courage to the point where they refuse to stand up for what's right because they know it may cost them money. Or worse, it will cost them an election.

SELF-PRESERVATION

When the abortion rights landmark case *Roe v. Wade* was overturned, many states like South Carolina rushed to put into place draconian legislation prohibiting abortion in nearly every case.

In 2023, a six-week abortion ban was making its way through the legislative process when five female senators joined together to put a stop to it. Three Republican and two Democratic women joined forces to filibuster and stop this legislation that would have effectively banned all abortions in South Carolina and allowed no exceptions for rape or incest.

One of the five, Republican Sen. Sandy Senn told NBC News, "We're not stupid. We certainly knew that as the Republican women that there could easily be [political] fallout." She was right. Sen. Senn and the other two female Republicans lost their following primary to Republican men, largely because of this stance. Now, in a state that is predominately Republican and at least half female, the South Carolina Senate will have no Republican female senators.

The courage these women showed, especially those Republicans who sacrificed their seats for their beliefs, has become increasingly rare, nearly extinct. With an increase in gerrymandering and an associated decrease in competitive elections, primary elections become the only race that politicians fear. As a result, they are much less likely to stand up to their own party for fear of losing the next campaign.

Sometimes it is not even about an issue, it is about a personality.

My predecessor and South Carolina's former governor, Mark Sanford, was the first casualty of this Trump era. He didn't say anything disrespectful or disparaging of Trump publicly; he just refused to kneel and kiss the ring. And when he disagreed with President Trump he would vocalize it. "Well, I would respectfully disagree with the President. . ." he would say. But with President Trump, it is 100 percent loyalty or nothing. As a result, President Trump took aim at Sanford in his 2018 congressional re-elect, endorsing Sanford's primary opponent, who ultimately edged him out in one of the largest upsets that cycle within the Republican primaries. That was the start of political casualties for Republicans who would not pledge 100 percent loyalty, 100 percent of the time.

The Democratic Party has been quick to criticize this blind loyalty by Republicans to Trump but slow to acknowledge the pervasive problem that exists on their own side. Despite the large number of voters who did not want Biden to run for re-election, members of Congress remained silent. I first called for him to not run in June 2022 and reiterated the position in an op-ed in early 2023. But aside from Congressman Dean Phillips, the Democratic caucus was mum on Biden and his reelection campaign.

It would not be until July 2024, less than four months before the election, when Democrats would finally acknowledge the dire situation the party, and country, was in with Biden leading the ticket. It is likely no coincidence that most stayed quiet through their own primary process because any opposition to Biden would be viewed as a betrayal of the party and might invite a primary opponent. While that may have been the fear, I do not view it as reality. Oftentimes, we, politicians especially, view social media as real life. It's not. Simply because something is trending or popular online doesn't mean that viewpoint is widely shared. The first elected officials to call for Biden to step aside, just a few months before the election, were skewered online. Yet, their viewpoint was widely shared with Democrats and Americans, despite what social media comments might indicate.

We have witnessed a vanishing of courage among our politicians and Democrats are as guilty as anyone. Americans seek leaders who will stand up for what's right no matter the consequences. If we expect the bare minimum from Democrats, the bare minimum is what we will continue to get. Most Democrats refused to make a comment on Biden out of fear it might cost them their seat. And while most do it for self-preservation, many do it to just go along. It is tough to go against the grain, to risk losing friends and being ostracized from the party. It is much easier to go along and get along.

LOSING FRIENDS

My affiliation with the bipartisan group No Labels became public when I penned an op-ed for *The Post & Courier* on May 12, 2023. This was eighteen months before Trump easily vanquished Harris. The title read "With Biden trailing Trump, we need a third option for President in 2024." In it, I wrote, "The national Democratic Party assumes foolishly that all moderates will automatically side with Biden over Trump, even though Democrats have done nothing to court these moderates." Looking back at the article, the entire summary of the failures of the Democratic Party were 100 percent true. It pains me to this day how the writing could be so clear upon the wall and no one in Democratic leadership cared to see. I was proud to take a stand, even though I knew it would be unpopular. However, I was not prepared for the nasty and personal onslaught of attacks that followed.

Minutes after the article went up online, texts started rolling into my phone. The DNC Chair, who I had considered a friend, engaged in a healthy back and forth with me over text. He never called. Donors of mine in Charleston also called and texted, lamenting their dismay with me and how my efforts would only help put Trump back in office. Leaders in political groups that once supported me as well as others felt the need to express their opinions to me, unsolicited of course. I was fielding texts for days. Ghosts from my political past, folks I had not heard from in years, felt the need to rise from their grave and reach out to me about their version of a political doomsday.

We are all human. It bothered me. But, the truth is it bothered me much less than it would have others. Some daggers came from those I would have considered friends. They came to my kids' birthday parties. We shared dinners and laughs, exchanged holiday texts. But if I had wondered where the line of friendship was, I found it at not supporting the president from our same party.

"I sure don't like your recent op-ed or agree with it in any way. Surprised. While I share some of your analysis of the problems, I sure don't share your solution. Not sure what you're thinking about No Labels. Truly. No need to respond."

Some of the texts were so obnoxious and persistent, I was left with no other option than to block them. It was sad that so many good people were completely blind to the reality and ignored all polls about the sentiment toward Biden running for a second term. I had rarely been more confident in anything than in my belief that Biden would not beat Trump. While I knew history would prove me correct, at the time and while going through this, I simply had to hold my tongue. Engaging with any texts, emails, or calls proved to be a colossal waste of time. People would simply have to wait and see.

Shortly after my op-ed was published, I spoke with my good friend, Chris Kenney, an attorney in Columbia, South Carolina. I knew Chris well. He was an extremely sharp attorney and involved in Democratic politics—a true asset. His girlfriend, Lindsey, had worked on my communications team when I ran for governor in 2022. Both were extremely good people with talents to match.

"How's it going?" Chris had asked me. "Well, it's been a tough slog since I ran the op-ed. Tons of folks coming out of the woodwork to take shots at me. Kinda disappointing to be honest."

"Well, hate to tell ya, bud, but it's getting ready to be a bit tougher," he said. "I've submitted a response to your op-ed, and *The Post and Courier* is running it tomorrow or the next day."

I thanked him for the heads up. It was a true class act by Chris to give me notice. A reflection of who he is as a person, but also emblematic of the legal profession from which we both come. There is an innate ability to separate the person from the argument, to remove the emotions and duke it out in the courtroom or, in this case, the newspapers and not make or take it personally in any manner. To this day, I still have a lot of respect for Chris for this because it is such a dying art. It's a hint of class that is almost completely gone in today's politics.

But class is a stranger in today's politics. Just like courage. Standing up to politicians or policies is certainly one way to demonstrate this quality. There was a time in the Democratic Party when leaders said what they believed and did not give a damn about the next election. There was a time when some would even put their bodies on the line. There used to be lions amongst us in the Democratic Party.

I served with one.

Back on March 7, 1965, my former colleague, the late Congressman John Lewis joined six hundred other peaceful protestors to march across the Edmund Pettus Bridge in Selma, Alabama. The protest was a response to the suppression of Black voters in the South and the recent killing of activist Jimmy Lee

Jackson by an Alabama state trooper. I cannot imagine what was going through my old colleague's head, or his blood, as he and others faced down local law enforcement while standing at the base of that bridge. As they attempted to cross it, a battery of weapons and violence was unleashed upon them. Tear gas was deployed and law enforcement swung bats and clubs at the unarmed protestors.

John Lewis had his skull cracked by a baton. The extraordinary bravery by Lewis and other protestors helped lead to the passage of the Voting Rights Act of 1965, aimed at eliminating racial discrimination at the ballot box. Their courage made a real difference.

In 2020, I had the honor of attending the annual march on the Edmund Pettus Bridge. Flanked by other politicians, we walked from the base of the bridge, up to the top and stopped right in the middle. Lewis, who had been diagnosed with pancreatic cancer the previous December was driven out to the middle of the bridge where he slowly exited the vehicle and stood as others gathered around him, cheering and taking pictures. It would be his last march across that bridge. It was a powerful moment for me to be there firsthand, trying my best to conceptualize all the emotions that would have captured those protestors as they stood up for what they believed in.

I think about John Lewis a lot. I think about the strength and courage that he possessed. I think about where the Democratic Party once stood, what it fought for, who it fought for and how hard it fought. When it had life.

And I always return to one thought: How far we've fallen.

11

THE POWER IN ONE

Each time a man stands up for an ideal, or acts to improve the lot of others ... he sends forth a tiny ripple of hope.
—ROBERT F. KENNEDY

Back in June 2025, I went on Fox News to discuss the plight of the Democrats. Joining me was conservative commentator Luke Ball. Observing the Democrats' losses in 2024, he remarked, "The Israelites wandered in the wilderness for forty years...and the Democrats are on track to beat that record." My friend, Luke, may have been a tad hyperbolic, but the party will not make it out overnight. It took many years for the Democratic Party to earn the stereotypes it has. The backslide will continue if nothing is done. Lessons will continue until they are learned.

Afford me some leeway to address what has not been fleshed out in this book and why.

Some may flip through these pages and complain there are not enough policy points to make up a platform on which a Democrat can successfully lead the party or turn the nose of the ship. I've addressed kitchen table issues that have been and remain important to voters. More will arise as time marches on.

Yet, there are fundamental cracks in the Democratic Party that first must be repaired before building vertical. Delivery matters, but the messenger and their credibility matter most. So to go straight to the Democratic platform without first addressing how the party can better connect with voters is putting the cart in front of the horse.

Others who read this will be disappointed that I have not spread the blame quite far enough.

Republicans are even worse.

What about Donald Trump?

What about the same problems on their side?

As mentioned from the onset, this is and remains about self-reflection. The Democratic Party has spent too much time focusing on President Trump's shortcomings instead of addressing its own. The Party has spent a decade incessantly bashing him. This tactic has long lost its usefulness and the only thing we have to show for it is a President Trump—twice! A new approach is desperately needed. And it starts by looking inward and changing the things that turn voters off.

The Republican Party will stumble. They will push issues too far. Ultimately, independents will seek out another option, and it is the responsibility of the Democratic Party to repair its flaws so it can resemble a suitable home for those disenfranchised.

Otherwise, apathy will wash over those voters and they will sit on the sidelines during elections, ceding more ground to partisans.

There are large threats to our democracy, some of which deserve more attention than the number of words I have allocated in this book.

I've touched on partisan gerrymandering, but how elections are carried out in our country is far from democratic. Redistricting, straight-ticket voting, and other restrictions are just to name a few. One of the biggest travesties affecting free and fair elections was in the case of *Citizens United v. Federal Election Commission* that permitted money to masquerade as free speech. It allowed unlimited amounts of cash to affect our elections, and the only beneficiaries are the winning candidates and the media that profits off their spending. Everyone else loses.

Our media has and continues to be the largest dividers of the American people. Turn on any "news" station in the evening and you will find it slanted with bias, amplifying voices that seek only to degrade those across the aisle. Neither side can agree on the problem, much less the solution. Yet, they know what sells. Media knows what keeps people tuned in, and entertainment has replaced information.

Social media is catching up fast. Its algorithms alienate us, pit neighbor against neighbor all while padding their bottom line. In an era where we are awash in information, there is a drought of knowledge. On any issue, "experts" have a platform to give their opinion and the more outlandish the theory or explanation, the faster it spreads.

In 2025, a photo went viral that was allegedly taken from the Mars rover of the nighttime sky as seen from the surface of the red planet. It was a stunning picture of countless stars and constellations of varying colors and brightness. Simply mesmerizing. Unfortunately, simply fake, too. I had done a cursory online search after a friend had posted it and sent them a message to let them know the picture, unfortunately, was bogus. Their response: *I don't care. It's a cool picture.* It was a reminder that we sometimes repost and reshare things that aren't true, but we do so because they fit our beliefs or narrative. It has become true with politics as well.

Admittedly, it is incredibly difficult to police what is correct and what is blatantly false all while respecting the First Amendment. However, elected officials and those running for office should be held to a higher standard to do a cursory search to determine whether a story or fact they share on social media bears any truth. We should all expect more of them. We do have many challenges in front of us. But before marching forward, the Democratic Party must tie its own shoes correctly (or best we can). It must re-establish its credibility before selling its vision to the American people. I believe in this as much as I believe in gravity itself.

I served alongside some incredible and noble leaders. Smart, competent individuals purely driven by the desire to make the lives of their constituents better and our country a more prosperous one. I also served with some whose motives and actions I found highly questionable. I have witnessed my old colleagues who began with the noble intention of working with others, seeking out compromise and building a legacy for themselves, while a brighter future for their kids. Yet, for too many, something happens along the way.

Many find the power and fame intoxicating. Going on TV and having your friends or family excited to see you on there can be exhilarating. Witnessing your followers on social media build and your reach extend feels invigorating and, suddenly, the priorities of fame and change are flip-flopped. The constant headlines, online chatter, cable news all become addictive and to continue feeding that obsession, politicians find they must have more extreme or divisive opinions, because that is what sells. Those tweets translate to headlines, which are then packaged into a fundraising email that solicits an attack from your opponents to which you feel compelled to respond. And the cycle continues.

Even the best, caring politicians who offered themselves up for public service with the purest of intentions, can fall victim to this addiction to fame. They originally set out to fix government. They try valiantly but become distracted along the way by the glitz and glamour of publicity. Some point in their career—or one evening—they go to bed being part of the solution and then wake up being part of the problem.

It seems that over the last few years, public office holders have lost their sense of legacy. And with that loss has gone its prime ingredient: courage.

Legacy is generally defined as "the lasting impact, reputation, or contribution someone leaves behind…what people remember about them and how their actions continue to shape our future." Those examples of people showing courage in this chapter, all leave a legacy that will remain long after they are gone. Even with the swift passing of time, I'm still writing about them. But…office holders today care more about the imperial and empty status as office holder than what to do with that office. Priority has shifted from legacy to reelection.

To build a legacy, has become too much work. Too much blood to shed. Too much courage. Meanwhile our country groans under the yoke.

It has often had me ponder the same question over and over.

Is Washington DC just a mere reflection of us, or are we a reflection of Washington DC? If it's the former, then we need to ask what *we* are willing to do to change the discourse and direction of not only the Party but the country. It can seem daunting—if not impossible—how each of us, individually, can change the enormous apparatus of politics or the rich media channels from which it is amplified. Yet, the truth is the strength of our democracy is ultimately in our hands and within each of us is the power to make a difference in shaping our party, our policy and, ultimately, our country.

The preamble in our country's founding document states, "We the People of the United States, in Order to form a more perfect Union... do ordain and establish this Constitution for the United States of America." Hence, the power of our government stems from the power of its people.

Despite the existence of gerrymandering, unlimited money in elections, or other flaws, voters are still able to collectively beat the odds. Yet, nothing happens collectively until it begins individually.

I'm reminded of a fairytale allegory that perfectly drives home this point.

There was once a giant forest fire raging through the dense woods. The wildlife was making their hurried way to get away from the flames. Antelope and deer bounded through the trees gracefully leaping their way to safety. Small varmints like the squirrel, rabbit, opossum, coon, and otter scampered across the forest floor. Even the majestic eagle was soaring high in the sky away from the billowing black smoke.

A wise old owl was making its lumbering way to safety when it stopped to rest on a limb. It then saw something that amazed him. He saw a little, tiny hummingbird flying to a nearby lake, yet untouched by the inferno. It would dip its little beak into the water and take a very small drop of water over to the roaring fire and, from a safe distance above, drop the little bit of water on the flame. The little hummingbird worked furiously—back and forth, back and forth—repeating this time after time. The wise old owl was aghast at this futile effort. Finally, he could remain speechless no more. He yelled at the little hummingbird with loud indignation and ridicule. "What in the world are you doing?" he asked. "Do you think your silly and meager little beak of water can do a thing to deter this enormous forest fire? Why are you doing this?"

The little hummingbird did not pause in its continual effort to drive back the fire. But it did answer the old owl: "I'm doing what I can."

Friends and family members have asked me why I wrote this book. My answer is the same as the little hummingbird. I'm doing what I can.

I was blessed to have served in Congress, having been one of the biggest upsets in my state's modern history. However, I currently hold no public office. I reside in a state that is controlled by the Republican Party. A state where even two of the largest cities—Columbia and Charleston—have seen their mayor's office swing from Democrat to Republican. Between the institutional challenges of gerrymandering and straight-ticket voting, a competitive race is hard to find in my home state.

But...I continue to do what I can. I still love my country, my state, and my community. And it pains me greatly to see what our leaders are doing: not leading. The Party plays the same ol' hymns: social security, Medicare, abortion, democracy. Americans are facing unprecedented challenges, mainly, finding it more and more expensive to stay alive. The Democratic Party will preach how it will "save democracy" or "fight climate change" while the average person just wants to raise a family without being shoved into bankruptcy.

Life was brimming in the Democratic Party when it could combine substance with soul. When it could listen, empathize with everyday struggles, breathe in those challenges and then exhale real, meaningful and bold solutions that would transform generations. It was when the Party was connected to the community because it respected and listened to it. In recent years, I've seen the Party drift further from the working class and, therefore, the solutions the Party espouses fall flat. The Party does not listen to voters and they've reciprocated.

Trust in our institutions—our government, judiciary, healthcare, and media—has been strained. Meanwhile, we are losing faith in our own individual ability to make a difference. We learn from our fairytale allegory, that the little hummingbird tried. Perhaps the bird simply wanted to make a statement to others that a threat was imminent and something must be done, even if the bird, itself, could not extinguish it.

On February 28, 1966, an old biplane rattled to a stop in Port Said, Egypt. Out stepped Abie Nathan, a former Israeli air force pilot, who said he wanted to talk with President Gamal Abdel Nasser about making peace with his country. Egyptian authorities arrested him and sent him back to Israel the next day. He failed, but became a beloved, if quixotic, figure in Israel from that day on. Nathan continued in his own meager way as a private citizen to promote peace in the Middle East, including a peace ship, anchored off the shores of Tel Aviv broadcasting music and messages of reconciliation. When he died at the age of eighty-one in 2008, he had the word "Nissiti" placed on his headstone. That is the Hebrew word for "I tried."

Efforts like this can be symbolic. They can be the catalyst that effectuates change. It may not be about the act, but about the spark it creates and what it ignites. It happens every day across this great country. Hope and optimism are contagious. It can begin with words that can prompt action. Elie Wiesel wrote, "Even words in moments of grace attain the quality of deeds."

Sen. Adam Schiff of California was telling me at dinner of firsthand stories he had heard from his constituents on the impacts of President Trump's ICE crackdown on illegal immigration. Local children born in the United States were not attending school because their parents, who may have been undocumented, would not drop them off or pick them up at school for fear of being detained by ICE. As a result, community members would pool together and take other parents' children to school, ushering them back and forth. Oftentimes, these kids were Americans but missing out on their education because of decisions their parents had made. So other Americans stepped up. Neighbors began looking after each other and everyday people were trying.

What is at stake is the life of the Democratic Party. But it goes far beyond that. Our country needs a strong Democratic Party as much as it needs a strong Republican Party and perhaps other strong parties. Competition breeds better ideas and policies. Iron sharpens iron. Governments ruled by one party miss out on the diversity of thought and the novel ideas that can stem from it.

It was us, as Americans, who gave our government its powers via our Constitution. As such, Washington DC reflects us, not the other way around, and if we wish to change it, we must start with ourselves. Changes within the Democratic Party start with changes within Democrats.

If we are to meet the challenges of our time, we must renew not just our Party but our faith in one another and in the democratic process itself. The strength of our nation has always come from spirited debate joined with a shared commitment to the common good. Let us restore that balance—to lead with ideas, to listen with humility, and to build a politics that inspires rather than divides. The future of our democracy depends on it, and together, we are more than equal to the task.

ACKNOWLEDGMENTS

Those who serve in office or run for office rely heavily on their staff. They are often the unsung heroes of much of the work accomplished. During my time in office and in campaigns, I had the great fortune to be surrounded by the best and brightest. They were dedicated to the greater mission to make our democracy better, day in and day out. It was not uncommon for me to take stances that were at odds with my own party. Yet, their unwavering loyalty and dedication to my work is what enabled all success I enjoyed. Without them, nothing would have been possible. Words alone cannot express the immense gratitude I feel toward those who worked in my campaigns, my congressional office and now at my law firm. I will forever be indebted to those who poured their hearts and souls into the noble calling that is public service. To all of those who have served and continue to serve a cause greater than themselves, I say thanks, thanks and forever thanks.